Entertaining Lives

by JANE CHURCHILL with EMILY ASTOR

Foreword by Bob Colacello

For Melissa

Entertaining Lives

Recipes from the houses of
Nancy Astor and Nancy Lancaster

by JANE CHURCHILL with EMILY ASTOR

Foreword by Bob Colacello

Photography by Andrew Montgomery

COPYRIGHT PAGE

First published in the UK in 2021 by Clearview Books
99 Priory Park Road, London NW6 7UX
www.clearviewbooks.com

Compilation © Clearview Books
Text © Jane Churchill & Emily Astor
Photography © Andrew Montgomery
Photography jacket background © Colefax & Fowler
Photography p9 © Elizabeth Winn, courtesy of Martin Wood
Photography p11 © Jane Churchill
Photography p14, p38, p66 © Getty Images
Photography p91 © Henry Wyndham
Photography p112 © Isabella Tree
Photography p134 © the Estate of Valerie Finnis, courtesy of the RHS Library, Wisley

ISBN: 978 1908337 542

Editor: Catharine Snow
Art Direction & Design: Charlotte Heal
Food styling: Jake McConville
Consultant and props: Jane Churchill
Production: Rosanna Dickinson
Colour reproduction: Pixywalls, London

Printed in Europe

CONTENTS

If taste could be inherited, Jane Churchill, one of London's most prominent interior designers for more than four decades, was born with a fortune. Nancy Astor was her great-great aunt, and the grandmother of Emily Astor, co-author of this book. Nancy Lancaster was also Jane's great-aunt. Both women were renowned hostesses of their time and are still revered as icons of style to this day. This book pays homage to them, their accomplishments and their way of life. It also explains what made these particular women so important, so influential and, let's not forget, so amusing. It's a story told through their recipes, their approach to entertaining, and Jane's memories of growing up in their legendary English country houses.

"The Two Nancys," as they were sometimes referred to, were actually American, born in Virginia and raised near Charlottesville, at Mirador, the country seat of the family patriarch, Chiswell Dabney Langhorne, a railroads and tobacco tycoon. Langhorne and his wife, Nanaire Keene, had five daughters, celebrated as the Langhorne Sisters for their beauty and Southern belle charm. The eldest, Lizzie, married Thomas Moncure Perkins, a Richmond cotton broker. Nancy Lancaster was their daughter, as was Jane Churchill's grandmother, Alice Perkins Winn. "My grandmother and her sister Nancy Lancaster were very close," Jane notes. "They fought like cats and dogs, but adored one another. Both lived till they were 97. Strong American women - that's where my blood comes from."

If anyone fits that description, it's Nancy Astor. In 1906, she married Waldorf Astor, the second Viscount Astor, and the unbelievably rich heir to much of his famous American grandfather John Jacob Astor's real estate, lumber and fur empire, which placed her at age 27 in the center of Britain's highest aristocratic and political circles. As a wedding present, Waldorf's father, William Waldorf Astor, who had transplanted the family from New York to England, gave them Cliveden, a vast estate dating back to the 1600s, set above the Thames an hour outside London. In 1919, Nancy became the first woman elected to Parliament, where she would remain until 1945, and continued hosting the lavish weekend house parties for what came to known as the Cliveden Set, mixing top Conservative Party politicians with the likes of Charlie Chaplin, Rudyard Kipling, George Barnard Shaw, Edith Wharton, and T.E. Lawrence (aka Lawrence of Arabia.)

"One my earliest memories is of Christmas at Cliveden when I was four," recalls Jane. "Nancy Astor died when I was 16 and she had kept every single thank-you note from my brother Henry, my sister Melissa and me for presents she had given us over the years. She was a big influence."

For her part, Nancy Lancaster was said to have "the finest taste of almost anyone in the world." Indeed, she would come to be seen as the most influential interior decorator of her generation and, as a partner in Colefax & Fowler, was credited with upgrading and promoting the traditional English country house look. In 1920, she married Ronald Tree, a scion of Chicago's Marshall Field department store dynasty, but who had been born and raised in England. In

1933, they bought Ditchley Park, in Oxfordshire, an enormous stately pile built in 1722 for the 2nd Earl of Lichfield and designed by James Gibbs. Working with Lady Sybil Colefax and Stephane Boudin of the Paris firm Jansen, she set about transforming Ditchley into the most stylish house in England.

In the late 1940s, the Trees divorced, and Nancy wed Lt. Colonel Claude Lancaster. In 1954, a year after that marriage dissolved, Nancy bought Haseley Court, an early 18th century manor house near Oxford, which she renovated and decorated with John Fowler. Jane was seven years old at the time, and from then on "we spent every school holiday at Haseley. Those days were the highlight of our year." As for the fabulous Lancaster entertaining style: "It wasn't so much lavish, as well put together. And delicious. It wasn't over rich, just very good - both my grandmother's and Nancy's, neither of whom could boil water."

Jane's mother had continued the Langhorne tradition of marrying into the English aristocracy, in her case to the Honorable Mark Wyndham, younger brother of Lord Egremont of Petworth, Sussex, And, in 1970, Jane herself wed Lord Charles Spencer Churchill, a cousin of Winston Churchill, and a grandson of the American heiress Consuelo Vanderbilt, later Consuelo Spencer-Churchill, Duchess of Marlborough. Meanwhile, Jane's career at great-aunt Nancy Lancaster's firm, Colefax & Fowler, led her to launch Jane Churchill Design in 1982, where, over the years, her client list has come to include everyone from the Crown Prince of Malaysia to cosmetics queen Estee Lauder.

I asked Jane Churchill if the famous line, "Living well is the best revenge" – attributed to the 16th century Church of England clergyman and metaphysical poet George Herbert, and used by Calvin Tomkins as the title of his 1971 biography of the Roaring Twenties icons Gerald and Sara Murphy – could be applied to her ancestors, the legendary Two Nancys. "They didn't need revenge. They had what they wanted. They just lived well. They loved to entertain the family. That was their raison d'être."

Bob Colacello, New York, July 2021

RIGHT: Drinks on the terrace at Haseley Court, from left to right: Nancy Lancaster, Nancy Astor and Cecil Beaton

Nancy Astor was thirteen years old when her father, Chiswell 'Chillie' Dabney Langhorne, having at last restored the family fortunes after the Civil War, bought Mirador, an Antebellum house in Greenwood, near Charlottesville, Virginina in 1892. It was here in 1897 that her niece, Nancy Lancaster, was born in the small cottage adjacent to the main house. For both women, Mirador was to exert a lifelong influence; a place where family and friends gathered, fast horses were fearlessly hunted and the hallways rang with gaiety and commotion. Infusing the proceedings was Chillie's propensity for lavish, Southern hospitality and his wife Nanaire's talent for creating beautiful yet comfortable interiors. When both Nancy Astor and Nancy Lancaster later moved to England, this code – of luxurious simplicity – was the one they lived by and Mirador the house to which they would return, year after year, to imbibe the true spirit of their childhoods. "Ever since I was old enough to reason", Nancy Lancaster would say, "all of the fun and glamour and excitement of life came from Mirador."

Mirador, with its 'shutters and breeze-gathering porches and its red-brick walls' lay at the foot of the Blue Ridge Mountains and was built in what, until 1800, had been Native American territory. The dogwood and honeysuckle, hazy grass meadows and apple orchards with the low-lying, tree-covered hills that slid into them from a distance, created a uniquely intimate and reassuring environment. It was remote, with red clay roads passable only with mules in bad weather, but Chillie, through his work for the C&O Railway, had the No 4 Express, which would normally whistle through, stop at the Greenwood station three miles away. It was this connection to civilization that brought down hordes of guests from Washington and New York.

The house itself was built on the classic Virginia plan, with each floor containing four large rooms, two on either side of a wide hall. To this, Chillie added wings for his large family: There were outbuildings for servants, a smoke house, dairy, an old barn and a brick cottage, used as an office and later as a nursery for the grandchildren. There were stables filled with horses, a kennel of foxhounds in the field behind the cottage, a tennis and a squash court. The garden, surrounded by a picket fence, had two squares for flowers and behind was the vegetable garden, orchards and fields to the Blue Ridge Mountains. Fruit and vegetables were pickled and made into jams. The home farm supplied eggs, milk, cream, chickens and turkeys. The smoke house was where Mirador's pigs were cured and turned into hams and bacon, while shooting for game – rabbit, deer, partridge, quail and geese – was a favourite sport which all the family enjoyed.

Chillie was passionate about food and how it should be cooked and passed this on to all his daughters. Most of the recipes in this book are taken from a hand-typed volume hand-bound in morocco and red cloth, with 'The Mirador Cookbook' embossed in gold lettering on the spine and the initials W.A (Waldorf Astor) on the front. This was Nancy Astor's copy, and now belongs to the authors' families, but it seems that more were distributed as Isabella Tree,

Nancy Lancaster's granddaughter, has hers to this day, at Knepp Castle.

This book was the foundation stone of their entertaining. Nancy Astor later wrote of her childhood and youth in Virginia, 'I think we were very sensibly fed, with good plain food and plenty of it.' Her approach was to mix up the colourful Southern cooking of her youth with the traditional English and French cuisine then found. Combined with the wit, charm and acerbity that both women were famous for, we can begin to appreciate the style in which they entertained, how entertaining they were and how many were entertained by them in return.

OPPOSITE: Mirador House, Albemarle County, Virginia, seat of the Langhorne family. The Trees purchased the house in 1922 from Nancy's Aunt Phyllis, and hired the New York architect William Delano to transform the house and gardens into a Georgian revival mansion, seen here in 1926.

CHAPTER 1

NANCY LANCASTER

"We're a family that says everything

and anything but never goes to

bed angry ... tears and screams,

then laughter and kissing. But other

people are simply horrified by it."

FIRST COURSES

'Dearest Aunt Nancy' wrote Elizabeth Winn to her great-aunt Nancy Astor in 1947, 'I've never really enjoyed Christmas since the ones when we were all at Cliveden before the war- I keep thinking of them all the time. We always had to play French & English in the afternoon below the terrace, and charades after tea and dressing up for dinner. All that seems to be a thing of the past... also I adored all the teasings and rows and Jakie's loud laugh. You must say it was fun.'

Nancy Astor was the first of the Langhorne sisters to make her permanent home in England when she married Waldorf Astor in 1906, and Cliveden, the huge Astor estate near Taplow in Berkshire, was their wedding present. Their London house was at 4, St James's Square (now the In & Out Club) and it was at these two locations that most of the parties were held. Long before she became the first female Member of Parliament in 1919, Nancy had to entertain for Waldorf, who was then the Member of Parliament for Plymouth Sutton, the seat that Nancy won in the by-election after her husband was granted a Peerage. "Waldorf and I did a great deal of entertaining. We were young and

had a great many friends", recalled Nancy, "What wonderful parties those at Cliveden were. Kipling, Kaiserling and Hillaire Belloc were frequent visitors." She remembered too the "immense charm" of Queen Marie of Roumania, who "said she would like to come and dine with us...so I just asked my own friends along, and we had Anna Pavlova to dance for us in the ballroom. How difficult it is to give any true picture of the gaiety and glitter of those pre-war London seasons."

It was an overwhelming task at first. Her father-in-law had retreated to Hever Castle in Kent, taking most of the staff with him. Cliveden needed a complete overhaul, and there were times when even the energetic Nancy would take to her bed with exhaustion. However, drawing on her mother's impeccable taste at Mirador, and her familiarity with modern American conveniences, Nancy took control of the decoration. She tore up mosaics and replaced them with wood, installed French furniture and comfortable sofas. She enlarged bedrooms, installed bathrooms, built bookcases and put in chintz curtains and covers. She did up the dining room with its Louis XV boiseries (seen on p76-77), which she had shipped over from the Chateau d'Asnieres in Paris. She filled the gloomy house with cut flowers, arranged in large bowls in the Virginian style – a look of 'organised chaos', which quickly caught on in England. She was, consciously or not, recreating all she had grown up with at home, introducing a blast of air into the stuffy drawing rooms of the Edwardian age. This aesthetic would later be developed into an art form by her niece, Nancy Lancaster.

Echoes of Virginia permeated everything. Once the decorating and staff were in place Nancy's eclectic hand could be felt as the menus and guest lists were rearranged – something that again, years later, Nancy Lancaster would emulate. "I like to throw things together and see how they get along" she would say, and in this she was lucky to have probably the finest butler in the land – Edwin Lee, known as 'Lord Lee of Cliveden' – to smooth over any disruptions. As her maid, Rosina Harrison was to recall, 'there was one particular thing about parties that always seemed to get her ladyship and Mr Lee hot under the collar: that was the size of the chairs and the seating accommodation. Her ladyship would insist on getting as many people round a table as possible and this gave little room for manoeuvre either for the guests of the footmen. Mr Winston Churchill always complained. One particular night he refused to eat anything and at the end he said,"Thirty dishes served and no damn room to eat one."'

Nancy's aim was to inject spontaneity and informality into her parties. As Arabella Boxer writes in her iconic book English Food: 'There were two significant outside influences on our food during this period: yet they had lasting effects and would have spread further had it not been for the outbreak of war. The first came from the United States...like Nancy Astor and Emerald Cunard who had married before the First World War. Many of these young women were talented exponents of the minor arts: interior decoration, entertaining and clothes. Almost without exception, they seemed to have a social ease and a lack of shyness which Englishmen found irresistible.'

OPPOSITE: Christmas at Cliveden 1921, from left to right: Waldorf Astor, Bill Astor, Bobbie Shaw, David Astor, Nancy, Michael Astor and Phyllis Astor.

Parsley Soup

Serves: 6
Prep time: 10 min
Cook time: 30 min

2 tbsp oil for frying,
  e.g. vegetable or sunflower
1 large or 2 small onions, sliced
750g/5 ¼ cups potatoes, peeled
  and diced
2 celery sticks, diced (optional)
40g/ ¾ cup chopped parsley
1.2 litres chicken or veg stock
Crème fraîche or double cream,
  to serve
Salt and pepper

Heat the oil in a large saucepan, then add the onions and fry on a low heat for 10 minutes, stirring every now and again, until soft (do not allow to burn). Add the potatoes, celery and half the parsley.

Add the stock, bring to the boil, reduce the heat and simmer for 10-15 minutes, until the potatoes are soft. Add the rest of the parsley and blitz in a food processor in batches or, much easier, with a hand blender in the saucepan.

Add a little more stock or water to thin if needed. Season with salt and pepper to taste, then reheat gently. Add a swirl (or dollop!) of crème fraîche or double cream to serve.

Avocado & Courgette Soup

Serves: 4
Prep time: 10 mins
Cook time: 30 mins

2 tablespoons olive oil
1 small onion, diced
4 garlic cloves, roughly chopped
2 large courgettes/zucchini, diced
2.5 – 3 cups stock/about 800ml (vegetable or chicken)
4 large basil leaves
1 large ripe avocado, diced
1 lemon
Salt and pepper
Croutons (optional)

Heat a large saucepan over medium/high heat. Add the olive oil, onion and a pinch of salt and pepper and cook for about 3 minutes. Add the garlic and cook for 1 min.

Add the courgettes/zucchini, ½ teaspoon salt and ¼ teaspoon pepper and cook for 5-7 minutes. Add the stock (start with 2.5 cups, you can always add more at the end). Bring to a boil then simmer for 5 minutes.

Turn off heat and add the basil, avocado, juice of 1 lemon, ½ teaspoon salt and pinch of pepper.

Transfer soup mixture (in batches) to a high powdered blender and blend until smooth. You can also use a handblender and blend it right in the saucepan. If soup is too thick add a little more stock to thin it out. Add salt and pepper to taste and serve topped with avocado and croutons. Soup can be served hot or chilled.

Tomato & Okra Soup

Serves: 6
Prep time: 10 mins
Cook time: 30 mins

2 tablespoons olive oil
1 large onion, chopped
1 red bell pepper, chopped
1 cup/ 100g chopped celery
2 cloves crushed garlic
1 litre vegetable or chicken stock
4 cups/ 800g chopped fresh tomatoes (about 3 large ones)
2 cups/ 400g sliced fresh okra
¼ cup/ 100g sliced fresh basil
2 teaspoons fresh thyme leaves
1 teaspoon hot sauce
1 teaspoon ground black pepper
1 teaspoon ground cloves
1 teaspoon salt

The original Mirador recipe calls for 'a peck of ripe tomatoes' which turned out to be about 20lbs of them, clearly the cook made this in quantity to put up in jars until needed. Often this was added to other vegetable soups to enhance the flavour.

In a large saucepan, heat olive oil over medium heat. Add onion, pepper, celery, and garlic. Cook, stirring occasionally, over medium heat, for 7 minutes. Stir in the stock and all remaining ingredients, and bring to a boil. Reduce heat, and simmer, uncovered, for 30-40 minutes or as long as the soup begins to thicken.

Black Bean Soup

Serves: 4-6
Prep time: 10 mins
Cook time: 45 mins

6 slices smoked streaky bacon
1 large onion, diced
3 cloves garlic, crushed/minced
400ml/ 2 cups chicken stock/broth
    pinch of dried oregano
    pinch of cayenne pepper
½ teaspoon ground cumin
    salt
2 x 400g or 14.5oz cans of black beans
14.5 fl oz water
½ teaspoon ground black pepper
Garnish
2 tablespoons chopped spring onions
    (scallions)
3 tablespoons sour cream

Place bacon in a cold pot. Turn heat to medium, cook and stir until the bacon is cooked but not crisp. Stir in onion; cook and stir for 5 minutes, until the onion turns translucent and golden.

Stir in garlic; cook for 2-3 minutes. Add chicken stock, turn heat to medium-high. Stir in oregano, cayenne and salt. Add black beans and water. Return to a simmer.

Simmer on medium-low, stirring occasionally, for 20-30 minutes. While it's cooking, mash about half the beans to thicken the soup.

Stir in black pepper and cumin. Add salt to taste.
Serve garnished with chopped green onions, and sour cream.

Clarified Beetroot Soup

Serves: 6
Prep time: 30 mins
Cook time: 45 mins

450g/3 cups raw beetroot
1 litre of good chicken stock
100ml/ ½ cup double/heavy cream
1 egg

Peel and slice the beetroot finely, season the stock with salt and pepper and cook gently in a saucepan filled with the chicken stock until tender. This should take around 30 minutes. Strain the beetroot and stock through a sieve or colander, reserving the stock in a fresh saucepan and discarding the beetroot.

To clarify the stock, separate the egg (discard the yolk or save for another use). In a small bowl, combine the egg white with ¼cup (50ml) of cold water. Stir the mixture into the hot, strained stock. Bring to boiling. Remove from heat and let stand for 5 minutes. (As the egg white cooks, it will coagulate and trap fine particles from the stock). Place a large sieve or colander, lined with several layers of damp, 100% cotton cheesecloth or muslin over a large bowl. Pour the stock through the cloth to strain out the particles and egg white.

To serve: Check seasoning, whip the cream and add separately to decorate the soup. A sprinkling of parsley or chives over the top can be added.

Clam Chowder

Serves: 4
Prep time: 15 mins
Cook time: 25 mins

1 tbsp vegetable oil
1 large onion, chopped
100g/ ½ cup chopped streaky bacon
1 tbsp plain (all purpose) flour
600ml/ 2 ½ cups fish stock
225g/ 1 ¼ cups new potatoes, halved
  pinch of mace
Pinch of cayenne pepper
300ml milk
320g/ 1 ½ cups any fresh and
  smoked fish
250g/ 1 cup cooked mixed shellfish
4tbsp single cream
Small bunch parsley, chopped
(Crusty bread to serve or crackers)

The recipe for the soup was obtained from the cook at Cedar Lodge, Rockport, Maine. This was where Charles and Irene Gibson would have stayed or dined waiting for the boat to take them to their island off Islesboro, Maine, known as 700 Acre Island on Dark Harbor. This soup is hearty enough as a main course for lunch, and only a small amount would be served as a first course at dinner.

Heat the oil in a large saucepan over a medium heat, then add the onion and bacon. Cook for 8-10 mins until the onion is soft and the bacon is cooked. Stir in the flour, then cook for a further 2 mins.

Pour in the fish stock and bring it up to a gentle simmer. Add the potatoes, cover, then simmer for 10-12 mins until the potatoes are cooked through.

Add the mace, cayenne pepper and some seasoning, then stir in the milk. Tip the fish mix into the pan, gently simmer for 4 mins. Add the cream and shellfish, then simmer for 1 min more. Check the seasoning. Sprinkle with the parsley and serve with some crusty bread or crackers.

Maryland Crab Soup

Serves: 8
Prep Time: 15 mins
Cook time: 45 mins

2 x 400g(14.5oz) tinned tomatoes
700ml/ 3 cups water
75g/ 1cup butter beans, cooked
160g/ 1 cup frozen corn
130g/ 1 cup sliced carrots
2 tbsp chopped onion
400ml/ 2 cups beef stock
450g/ 1 lb fresh crabmeat
10 crab claws, (optional)
4.5L/ 1 gallon water
1 tsp celery salt
1 tsp crushed red chilli flakes
1 tsp paprika
Salt and black pepper

Place the tinned tomatoes, water, lima/butter beans, corn, sliced carrots, chopped onion, spices (Marylanders - reach for the Old Bay Seasoning), and beef stock, in a large saucepan. Heat to simmer, cover, and cook for 5 minutes.

If you are using the crab claws, in a deep stockpot bring 4.5 litres/1 gallon water to boil. Add crab claws and boil 6 minutes. Drain crab and set aside. When cool remove the shells and extract the crabmeat inside.

Stir crabmeat (and crabs claws, if using) into tomato and vegetable mixture. Cover and simmer 10-15 minutes longer. Check for seasoning and add salt and a good grinding of black pepper. Serve hot.

Chicken Soup

Serves: 4
Prep time: 15 mins
Cook time: 35 mins

1 tbsp olive oil
2 onions, chopped
3 medium carrots, chopped
1 tbsp thyme leaves,
   roughly chopped
1.4L/ 6 cups chicken stock
300g/ 2 ½ cups leftover roast
   chicken, shredded
200g/ 1 ⅓ cups frozen peas

An excellent way to use up leftover roast chicken.

Heat the olive oil in a large heavy-based pan. Add the onions, carrots and thyme leaves, then gently fry for 15 mins.

Stir in 1.4l chicken stock, bring to a boil, cover, then simmer for 10 mins.

Add the leftover roast chicken, remove half the mixture, then purée with a stick blender. Tip back into the pan with the rest of the soup, the peas and seasoning, then simmer for 5 mins until hot through.

(If you like noodles in your soup, drop in a couple of handfuls once the peas are in, and simmer for 5 mins as per instructions).

Beef Consommé

Serves: 6-8
Prep time: 15 mins
Cook time: 2 hours

½ lb/ 225g lean beef
1 small carrot
1 small onion or leek
1.4L/ 3 pints good beef stock/broth
Bouquet garni
1 egg white

Shred the meat finely, and peel and chop the vegetables. Put all the ingredients in a large saucepan, adding the egg white last.

Heat gently, whisking continuously with a wire whisk, until a thick froth forms on the surface. Cease whisking, reduce the heat immediately and simmer the consommé very slowly for 1.5-2 hours. Do not let the liquid reach boiling point, as the foam layer will break up and cloud the consommé.

Strain the liquid into a bowl through a double layer of muslin, or a clean jelly bag. Strain it a second time through the egg foam left in the muslin, it should now be perfectly clear and sparkling.

To serve
Reheat the consommé and season to taste. Sprinkle a few chives or any green herb across the top if you have any. The addition of a poached egg is advised for a dinner party or lunch dish.

COLD SOUPS

Gazpacho

Serves: 4-6
Prep time: 10 mins
Cook time: 30 mins

1 cup green peppers chopped
    small (or one large green
    bell pepper)
5 large tomatoes
1 large cucumber
1 medium sweet onion
A few chopped leaves of
    sweet basil
10g/ ½ cup chopped parsley
¼ tsp garlic salt
3 tbs cut chives

Ingredients for dressing:
125ml/ ½ cup tarragon vinegar
185ml/ ⅔ cup olive oil
¼ tsp garlic powder
½ tsp salt
Plenty of freshly milled black
    pepper

Skin the tomatoes by running a sharp knife around their circumference so that the skin is pierced. Drop into a bowl of boiling water so that they are completely immersed. When the water is cool, remove the tomatoes and their skins should peel off in your fingers. Once skinned, finely chop and deseed the tomatoes and put to one side Finely chop the cucumber and sprinkle with ¼ tsp of salt and let it sit for an hour. Drain off most of the liquid. Finely chop the onion and chop and deseed the green pepper. When the above ingredients are ready, mix them all together with with the remaining ingredients, basil, parsley and garlic salt.

Then add the dressing to the bowl of mixed vegetables and herbs. Add 6 or 7 ice cubes and put in the fridge.

To Serve:

This seems to have been served as it was, but today's cooks prefer a liquidized version. After half an hour in the fridge, put all the ingredients into a blender or liquidizer and blitz to a smooth soup. If more liquid is required, add a little more water. Sprinkle the top with the chives and add a dollop of crème fraiche if desired.

Vichysoisse

Serves: 4
Prep time: 20 mins
Cook time: 25 mins

2 large leeks, white parts only,
    finely chopped
1 onion finely chopped
1 large potato, thinly sliced
30g/ 2 ½ tbsp butter
500ml/ 2 cups chicken stock
Salt and freshly ground black
    pepper to taste
250ml (12 fl oz) double cream
Chives to garnish

Melt the butter in a saucepan and add the chopped leeks, potatoes and onion. Stir to coat with the butter, then turn the heat to low, cover and cook for 10 minutes to allow the vegetables to soften and sweat down.

Add the stock, salt and pepper to taste and simmer with the cover on for a further 25 minutes.

Puree the mixture with a hand blender. Adjust seasoning and allow to cool.

When cool, stir in the cream and serve with a swirl of cream and chopped chives.

Spring Pea Soup

Serves: 6-8
Prep time: 20 mins
Cook time: 10 mins & 1 hr to chill

1 bunch spring onions (scallions)
  trimmed and roughly chopped
1 medium potato, peeled and diced
1 garlic clove, crushed
800ml/ 3 ¼ cups chicken stock
900g young pea in the pod
  (to give about 250g shelled peas)
  or simply 250g/ 6 cups frozen peas
4 tbs chopped fresh mint (reserve
  some for garnish)
1 tsp caster sugar (add more if the
  sweet/salt balance is out)
1 tbs fresh lemon or lime juice
150ml/ 1 ¼ cups buttermilk
  or sour cream
Salt and pepper to taste

Put the spring onions into a large pan with the potato, garlic and stock. Bring to the boil, turn down the heat and simmer for 15 minutes or until the potato is very soft. For the garnish, blanch 3 tbsp of the shelled (or frozen) peas in boiling water for 2-3 minutes, drain, put in a bowl of cold water and set aside. Add the remaining peas to the soup base and simmer for 5 minutes – no longer, or you will lose the lovely fresh flavour of the peas.

Stir in the mint, sugar and lemon or lime juice, cool slightly then pour into a food processor or hand blend with a liquidizing stick and whizz until as smooth as you like. Stir in half the buttermilk or soured cream, taste and season with salt and pepper.

To serve the soup cold, cool quickly, then chill – you may need to add more stock to the soup before serving as it will thicken as it cools. To serve hot, return the soup to the rinsed-out pan and reheat without boiling (to prevent the buttermilk or soured cream from curdling).

Serve the soup in bowls, garnished with the remaining buttermilk or sour cream, the drained peas and a scattering of the remaining chopped mint.

Cold Cucumber Soup

Serves: 6-8
Prep time: 30 mins
Cook time: 20 mins plus 1hr to chill

60g/ 4 ¼ tbsp
1 onion
1 clove crushed garlic
3 or 3 cups cucumbers peeled
  and diced
1.5L/ 4 ¼ cups chicken stock
150g/ ½ cup plain yoghurt
¼ cup or half a bunch chopped mint
¼ cup or half a bunch chopped dill
¼ cup or half a bunch chopped
  tarragon
2 lemons
100ml/ ⅓ cup single cream

Peel and dice the onion and roughly chop the cucumbers.

Melt the butter in a large pan and sauté the onions over a medium heat for 4 to 5 minutes, or until softened. Add the garlic and cucumber, reduce the heat to low and continue to cook for 5 minutes.

Add the stock, bring to the boil then reduce the heat again. Season well with sea salt and black pepper, and leave to simmer for 5 minutes. Chop and add the fresh herbs, squeeze in the lemon juice and cook for a further 5 minutes. Transfer to a blender, add the plain yoghurt, and purée until smooth (in batches, if necessary). Place the soup in a bowl, allow to cool at room temperature, then refrigerate until cold.

Whisk in the cream, season to taste, then serve.

Egg Mousse
(with Caviar & Melba Toast)

Serves: 4
Prep time: 1 hour
Chill time: about 4-5 hours,
preferably overnight

6 eggs
300ml/1 ¼ cups double/
   heavy cream
1 small glass sherry
1 clove garlic minced/crushed
Celery Salt
Black pepper
Garnish
Caviar (or lumpfish caviar)
Chives

A long forgotten but highly economical and delicious first course, often served as a light lunch dish with a green salad in the summer. You can either chill the mousse in a 1½ pint soufflé dish, or separately in dariole moulds as seen opposite.

Hardboil the eggs and chop them roughly. Beat the cream with an electric handwhisk until thick; flavour this with the crushed garlic, celery salt and black pepper to taste.

Stir in the eggs gently, and pour the mixture either into one soufflé dish, or the four dariole moulds.

Allow to set in the fridge for at least two hours. When set, if using the individual moulds, then run a knife carefully around the edge and turn out onto a serving dish.

Top with the caviar and chopped chives.

MELBA TOAST
Take one or two thick slices (per person) of white bread with the crusts cut off, and toast as normal. Split them in two and toast the uncooked middle sides under a hot grill.

Alternatively, cut stale bread into very thin slices, crusts off, and place them on a baking tray and dry them off in the bottom of the oven until crisp and curling at the edges.

Baked Eggs (En Cocotte)

Serves: 4
Prep time: 5 mins
Cook time: 10 mins

Butter to taste
4 individual ramekins
4 large eggs
8 tablespoons double/heavy cream
  (2 per ramekin)
100g/ 1 cup grated cheddar
  cheese
Salt and pepper to taste

The Edwardians consumed a vast number of eggs, and there are a vast number of recipes concerning them. They were normally served at breakfast and lunch, as is usual nowadays, and would not have appeared as an appetizer at dinner. However we have placed them in this chapter for convenience.

Preheat the oven to 180 C / Gas 4. Grease 4 small ramekin dishes and leave a knob of butter in each.

Break one egg into each of the four ramekin dishes followed by two tablespoons of double cream. Season with salt and pepper.

In a small bowl, combine the grated Cheddar cheese and sprinkle over each of the egg ramekins. Place the ramekins into a deep baking tray and pour boiling water up to half the depth of the ramekins.

Bake in the preheated oven for 10 minutes, or until the eggs are cooked. Remove the ramekins from the oven and serve immediately.

Mrs Gibson's Eggs

Serves: 6-8
Prep time: 30 mins
Cook time: 30 mins

10 hardboiled eggs
15 spring onions (scallions)
250g/ 2 ⅔ cups breadcrumbs
300ml/ 1 ¼ cups single cream
25g/ 2 tbsp unsalted butter
Salt and pepper to taste

Mrs Gibson was Irene Langhorne, third of the Langhorne children. This is still a family favourite.

Preheat the oven to 180 C/350 F/ Gas 4. Butter a baking dish.

Separate the egg whites from the egg yolks, putting each into a separate bowl. Chop up the egg whites finely, and gently crumble the egg yolks apart. Slice up the spring onions and fry in the butter until soft.

In the baking dish, put a layer of breadcrumbs, a layer of egg whites, a layer of egg yolks and a layer of onions, dot with butter, salt and pepper and continue layering until the dish is full.

Pour over the cream until the eggs are covered. Bake in the oven for about 20-30 minutes until the top is golden brown. Serve immediately.

Eggs Benedict

Serves: 4
Prep time: 30 mins
Cooking time: 30 mins

HOLLANDAISE SAUCE
4 egg yolks
A pinch of sea salt
180g/ ¾ cup unsalted butter
1 ½ tbsp lemon juice

EGGS BENEDICT
4 English muffins
4 large eggs
4 pieces smoked, free range ham
Hollandaise sauce

HOLLANDAISE SAUCE
Warm the container of a food processor by filling it with very hot water and allow to stand for 5 minutes. Drain and wipe dry. Put the egg yolks and salt into the container and cover with the lid, leaving the funnel open. Melt the butter over a low heat until almost boiling. Process the egg yolks for 30 seconds then add the butter through the funnel in a thin stream while continuing to process. The sauce should thicken, if not thick enough, transfer to a bain marie and continue stirring until it does. Add the lemon juice and serve warm.

EGGS BENEDICT
Fill a large pan just over one third full with boiling water and the vinegar. Bring the water to a simmer. One by one, crack the eggs into a small bowl and gently tip into the simmering water. Poach for 2–3 minutes. Remove with a slotted spoon. Toast the muffin halves and spread with butter. Put a muffin half on each plate and top with ham. Place an egg on top of each muffin and spoon over some hollandaise sauce, black pepper and chopped chives if to hand.

Eggs Mimosa

Serves: 20 mins
Prep time: 30 mins
Cook time: 45 mins

12 hardboiled eggs
75g/ ⅓ cup mayonnaise
75g/ ⅓ cup fresh chopped parsley
Salt and pepper to taste

Cut the hard-boiled eggs in half, lengthwise, and carefully remove the yolks. Divide them into two batches in separate bowls.

Yolks Batch 1: Mash the egg yolks, add some salt and pepper, then add just enough mayonnaise to make a smooth spread. Fill the egg white cavities with this spread.

Batch #2: Use a grater with the smallest holes (such as for lemon zest or grating nutmeg) and grate the other yolks in a bowl. (The smaller the grating hole, the fluffier the grated yolks.) Gently fold in a little more salt and pepper. Just before serving, sprinkle the fluffy egg-yolk mixture generously over the filled eggs and scatter the parsley over that.

Creamed Lobster

Serves: 4
Prep time: 10 mins
Cooking time: 30 mins

2 tablespoons butter
1 medium shallot, minced
2 tablespoons flour
1 cup (250ml) milk or half-and-half
   (whole milk & single cream)
1 cup (170g) cooked lobster meat
Salt and pepper
split biscuits, toast points, or baked
   puff pastry shells
Parmesan cheese, for garnish
Parsley, for garnish

Lobster with a creamy sauce and Parmesan cheese. Add a teaspoon or two of sherry to the sauce if you'd like.

Melt butter in a skillet (frying pan) over medium-low heat. Add shallots to the skillet (frying pan) and cook, stirring, until tender and lightly browned.

Stir the flour into the butter and shallots and continue cooking for 2 minutes.

Gradually stir the milk into the roux and cook, stirring, until thickened. Add a teaspoon or two of sherry if desired. Add the lobster and heat through.Taste and season with salt and pepper.

Serve over biscuits, toast points, or baked puff pastry shells. Garnish with Parmesan cheese and parsley, as desired.

Prawn Cocktail

Serves 6
Prep time: 20-40 mins
Cook time: 10 mins

2lb (900g) large uncooked
   prawns in their shells or
   cooked prawn equivalent
1 lettuce such as Cos/Romaine
1 ripe avocado
26g/ ¼ cup rocket (arugula)
   leaves
Cayenne pepper
1 lemon, divided into 6 wedges

FOR THE SAUCE:
1 small jar Hellmann's mayonnaise
1 dessertspoon Worcestershire
   sauce
A few drops of Tabasco
1 tsp soft brown sugar
1 dessertspoon lemon juice
Salt and pepper to taste

If using uncooked prawns, heat a large frying pan/skillet and dry-fry the prawns for 4-5 minutes until pink. When cool, reserve 6 in their shells for a garnish and peel the remainder. Then take a small sharp knife, make a cut along the back of each peeled prawn and remove any black thread. Place in a bowl, cover with clingfilm and keep in the fridge until needed.

Mix the sauce ingredients together in a bowl, checking for seasoning. Add the prawns and mix again. Shred the lettuce and rocket finely and divide between 6 glasses or plates, peel and chop the avodcado and divide among the 6 servings. Top with the prawns, dust with the cayenne pepper and garnish with one section of lemon and 1 unpeeled prawn per serving.

Scallops à la Meuniere

Serves 4
Prep time: 20 mins
Cook time: 10 mins

450g/ 1lb sea scallops
85g/ 6 tbsp butter
60g/ 4 tbsp chopped spring
   onions/scallions
1 large garlic clove, crushed
3 tbsp dry white wine
¼ tsp salt
1 dash cayenne pepper
2 tbsp finely chopped parsley
1 lemon

Rinse scallops in cold water; pat dry with paper towels. In a large frying pan, heat half the butter on a high heat until sizzling; add scallops. Immediately reduce heat to medium, and cook scallops 2 to 3 minutes per side until lightly browned, turning once.

Melt the rest of the butter in with the scallops then add the chopped spring onions and the garlic, tossing to coat and saute for 2 minutes. Add the wine and cook for 1 minute more. Remove from heat and season with salt and cayenne; sprinkle with the snipped parsley. Serve hot with a generous squeeze of fresh lemon.

Scrambled Eggs in Smoked Salmon Rolls

Serves 4
Prep time: 15 mins
Cook time: 20 mins

7 eggs
1 tablespoon of double/heavy cream
50g/ 3 tbsp butter
450g/ 1lb smoked salmon

Strain the lightly beaten eggs into a double boiler in which the butter has already melted. Season and scramble. When the eggs are beginning to set stir in the cream. Finish cooking and allow to cool. Lay out the slices of cold salmon and place the scrambled eggs on one side, and roll up. Serve cold but not chilled.

Mirador Herring Roes with Anchovy Butter

Serves 2
Prep time: 15 mins
Cook time: 20 mins

3 anchovy fillets
100g/ 7 tbsp butter
2 slices white bread,
  crusts removed
200g/ 7oz soft herring roe
1 tbsp cayenne pepper
Flour for dusting
1 tbsp vegetable oil
25g/ 1 ½ tbsp butter
1 lemon, quartered

Mash together the anchovies and half the butter until smooth, and set aside. Toast the bread and keep warm. Blanch the roes for 20 seconds in boiling water, drain, pat dry and roll in flour seasoned with salt and the cayenne pepper. Heat the oil and remaining butter in a frying pan until very hot, and fry the roes. Turn down heat and cook for 2 minutes and then turn over and repeat, until they are golden and slightly crisp on the outside. Lift out and drain on kitchen paper. Discard the butter and wipe out the pan. Lower the heat, add the anchovy butter, then the roes and cook for 30 seconds, then place on the toast and serve immediately with lemon wedges.

CHAPTER 2

NANCY LANCASTER

"Aunt Nancy, why don't you think

before you speak?"

NANCY ASTOR

"How do I know what I think until

I've said it?"

MAIN COURSES

'Only once did Mr Lee nearly leave the Astors, exasperated by the number of extra guests her Ladyship had invited at the last minute. He could stand it no more and one evening announced to her that he would be leaving at the end of the month. Quick as a flash her ladyship saw the danger she was in. "In that case, Lee, tell me where you're goin' because I'm coming with you."'

The recipes contained within the Mirador Cookbook at once strike the reader with their simplicity, informality and above all, flexibility. These dishes were created to feed a few or a crowd, so if guests turned up unexpectedly, as they often did in the South, they were required almost by law to stay for dinner if not the night. This level of hospitality was in complete contrast to the highly structured, exclusive and formal entertaining of the 1900s in England, in which hostesses sent out invitations months in advance.

BELOW: A weekend houseparty at Cliveden in 1928, from left to right Amy Johnson the international aviator, Charlie Chaplin, Nancy Astor, George Bernard Shaw.

This struggle between the old order and the new can clearly be seen in the confrontation between Nancy Astor and her butler; it must have been difficult conforming to such rigid standards at first. The staff were trained to show uninvited visitors the door, their name never to be uttered in the household again. Royalty was the exception. As Nancy later remembered, "One weekend we had a large houseparty at Cliveden, including the Duchess of Connaught, when King Edward suddenly rang and announced that he wanted to come over for lunch right there and then. He brought his entire household over with him, including Alice Keppel (the King's mistress) and Mrs Willie James, a famous society hostess. He must have enjoyed himself because he stayed until eight o'clock in the evening!'

Memories of Mirador, where there were always numerous mouths to feed and where the doors were permanently open to guests and passers by must have been difficult to erase. A plate of cinnamon teacakes was always on the table in the sitting room, with lady apples from the orchard in a basket in the hall and cherry cobblers or mint juleps waiting to mixed at sundown. Chillie had Captain Mickey, the conductor of the C&O express train, bring at his behest Chesapeake Bay oysters, Virginia spots and shad roe from Norfolk Bay every week. Spanish mackerel, soft shell crabs and terrapins from Baltimore found their way into these deliveries. 'Father kept the terrapins in the cellar, they used to walk around down there and Phyllis and I got greatly attached to them. When the terrible day of massacre came, we wept bitterly. But we ate the soup all right!' said Nancy.

The delicious, pale green soup for which the poor terrapins were sacrificed was a Southern delicacy but the Mock Turtle broth that was being offered in English dining rooms as an alternative provided risible contrast. Which was the culinary problem Nancy encountered; the luxurious simplicity of the food at Mirador did not exist in Britain, even though the same resources such as vast vegetable gardens, orchards and home farms were available to those owning large country estates. It had been abandoned in favour of pseudo-French cooking, an anglicised version of Gallic dishes adapted to banquets and grand dining but which omitted much of the essential qualities of the originals.

Despite the Virginian infusion, current trends prevailed, and the Astors still looked to the best French chefs. From 1909 until shortly before his death in 1914, Monsieur Papillion 'the finest of them all' according to Mr Lee, was the head chef at Cliveden. He was succeeded by Philéas Gilbert, who was equally celebrated and wrote several books, including *La Cuisine de tous les Mois* published in 1931. Gilbert was one of the three collaborators on Escoffier's *Guide Culinaire* and was ranked as gifted as his colleague by the Société des Cuisiniers de Paris. Nonetheless, it was hard to reconcile a Gilbert creation such as 'Poulards de Bresse a la Russe, sur Socle' with the Southern fried chicken and cream gravy that Nancy craved. "When we first went to Cliveden," she recalled, "I stood the chef's cooking for a while. Then I said 'Aunt Ada in Virginia could do better than this' and we reorganized the kitchens."

Corned Beef Hash

Serves: 4
Prep time: 10 days or 15 mins
Cook time: 15 mins

500g/ 3 medium sized potatoes
(peeled and chopped)
2 tablespoons melted butter
or vegetable oil
1 large onion (peeled and chopped)
340g/ 2 ¼ cups shredded corn
brisket or corned beef
200ml/ 1 cup beef stock
2 tablespoons Worcestershire sauce
Salt and pepper to taste

The Mirador kitchen, like its counterparts at Cliveden and Ditchley, would undoubtedly have made its own corn beef. This is not a difficult dish, as the term has nothing to do with corn, the yellow kerneled vegetable, but the English term for a small particle or granule, such as a grain of salt. In the days before modern refrigeration, salting meat was a way to preserve it and keep it from spoiling. This is a very economical recipe, as it uses brisket, one of the most inexpensive cuts of beef.

To make corn (or salt beef) is simple: brine the brisket in a mix of salt and water (1 ½ cups/200g to a gallon) with 4 teaspoons of curing salt and any spices you'd like to add, for up to a week/10 days in the fridge, in a tightly sealed container or freezer bag. Turn the meat every once in a while.

After that, rather like a ham, place the meat in a stockpot, cover with water and add spices that may include peppercorns, garlic, mustard, tarragon, thyme, parsley, cloves, and nutmeg. Simmer, covered, for at least 4 hours until the meat is tender and can be pulled apart.

Alternatively, simply buy a tin or can of corned beef at your local supermarket.

First of all boil the cubed potatoes until soft but not mushy. Chop the corn beef very fine and mix with the chopped onion and cooked potatoes. Add the vegetable oil or butter, whichever you prefer, add salt and pepper to taste, and mix again.

Put the mixture into a frying pan, and fry on a medium to low heat, 'very slowly'. During this process add the stock bit by bit until it is absorbed.

Serve with baked beans and some curly kale.

Roast Ribs of Beef

Serves: 4
Prep time: 10 mins
Cook time: 20 mins per kg/lb for rare,
25 mins per kg/lb for medium

1.7kg/ 3lb 12 oz boned and
   rolled fore ribs, wing ribs
   or sirloin, plus bones
150ml/ 1 ½ cups red wine

Preheat the oven to 220 C/428 F. While it heats, weigh the joint and calculate the cooking time (see recommendations above).

If using joined ribs as a roasting rack, tie the beef onto it with string. Or if separated, lay the ribs in the roasting tin, with the beef joint on top, fat side up. Roast for the first 20 minutes at even higher heat than above, then lower the oven to 180 C/355 F. For the rest of the time, baste the meat every 15 minutes. When the time is up, remove the beef, wrap loosely in foil and leave to rest. Drain off the fat from the tin, add the wine and cook over the hob, scraping up all the bits of sediment. Strain through a sieve into a jug, and when the beef has rested for 20 minutes, serve as a jus with the carved meat.

Brunswick Stew

Serves: 10-15
Prep time: 1hour
Cook time: Step 1: 2 hours, Step 2:
at least 4 hours (or 3 days)

1kg/ 3lbs large beef shanks
   on the bone
2 chickens (squirrels are better
   if you can get them)
220g/ 8oz fat ham, or old ham bone
1 red chilli pepper
Salt and black pepper
4kg/ 1 gallon stewed or tinned
   tomatoes
12 ears of corn
1kg/ 1 quart butterbeans (dry)
8 large onions, peeled and chopped
12 pods of okra
3 stalks celery
1 bottle tomato ketchup

This recipe was traditionally cooked in a cauldron over a live kitchen fire. Today a very large stockpot would be needed to fit all the meat ingredients into it.

Step 1: put all the ingredients into the stockpot with 2 gallons (9 litres) of water, or enough to cover the meat. Bring to the boil then simmer for about two hours until the meat is falling away from the bones. Cool then drain and bone the chickens and the beef. Remove the ham bone if using.

Step 2: Rinse the stockpot then place the boned meat, with all the vegetable ingredients, and to quote Mrs White the cook at Mirador ' I frequently cook this for three days' on a low heat.

Cotelettes à la Milanese

Serves: 4
Prep time: 15 mins
Cook time: 15 mins

4 bone-in veal cutlets
2 eggs
150g/ 1 cup breadcrumbs
100g/ 7 tbsp butter
Salt
1 lemon

Flatten the meat part of the cutlets with a mallet or rolling pin until as thin as possible (it helps to place them in between two sheets of clingfilm). Beat the eggs in a bowl and dip the cutlets in, holding them by the bone.

Press into a separate bowl of breadcumbs pressing down to ensure all the meat is covered. In a frying pan heat the butter. When it foams, add the cutlets and cook for 7-8 minutes on each side, making sure the butter doesn't brown. Sprinkle each side with salt. Serve with quartered lemon.

Gigot d'Agneau avec Flageolets

Serves: 6-8
Prep time: 15 mins
Cook time: 20 mins per 450g/lb

1.3kg/ 3lb leg of lamb
6 cloves peeled garlic
30g/ 2 tbsp butter
3 400g/14oz tins flageolet
  or cannellini beans, drained
  and rinsed
1 tbsp chopped fresh parsley
2 sprigs fresh rosemary
Salt & pepper to taste

Preheat the oven to 220 C/425 F.

Place the leg of lamb in a large baking dish. Make about 6 inserts into the meat, and push garlic cloves into them along with a sprig of rosemary. Brush butter over the lamb and season with salt and pepper. Put in oven and roast at high heat for 20 minutes, then lower heat to 180 C/355 F and arrange the beans round the lamb mixing to coat with the juices. Cook for the rest of the time according to the weight of the joint.

Remove lamb and let it rest for 10 minutes before carving. Arrange the beans on the side with chopped parsley sprinkled over.

Virginia Ham with Pickled Peaches

Serves: ham size dependent
Prep time: about 3 days
Cook time: 2-4 hours

FOR THE HAM

One uncured ham, the best quality
you can afford and any size.
A pot large enough to hold it (make
sure in advance)
Cloves
Brown muscovado sugar

PICKLED PEACHES

Also delicious with roast pork or
duck. You will need a 1 litre
sterilising jar, washed and dried
out in the oven to sterilise it.
8 large ripe but firm peaches
350 g granulated sugar
1 pint (570 ml) white wine vinegar
2 tablespoons fresh lime juice
1 level dessertspoon coriander
seeds
1 level dessertspoon mixed
peppercorns
3 shallots, peeled and finely sliced

'Nanaire was famous for her home-cured Virginia hams ... and generations on, family Christmas is not complete without Virgina ham 'sliced thin as smoked salmon' and Nancy Lancaster's pickled peaches'. Isabella Tree

HAM

Soak the ham in cold water for 24 hours. Then scrub it, and put in a fresh pot of cold water to boil. Once it has reached a boil reduce to a very slow simmer, so that you can hardly see the bubbles. Cover and cook for 25 mins to the lb or kg, but not less than 2 hours. When tender, take off the stove and leave it to cool in the liquid overnight. Skin the ham, leaving the underlayer of pale fat. Score this crosshatch with a sharp knife and press in whole cloves at the crossing of each hatch. Sprinkle thickly with muscovado sugar (some mix with molasses or black treacle but just the sugar is also fine).

Bake in oven at high heat until brown and bubbling (about 20 minutes). Remove from oven, and allow to cool. Serve with the peaches, and maybe some celeriac remoulade.

PEACHES

Begin by measuring the sugar, wine vinegar, lime juice, coriander seeds, peppercorns and shallots into a large saucepan or preserving pan.

Give everything a good stir, then place the pan on a low heat and allow to heat through, stirring from time to time until all the sugar has dissolved – don't let it come up to simmering point until all the granules of sugar have completely dissolved.

Put another saucepan of water on to boil. Halve the peaches and remove the stones, then drop them into the boiling water for a few seconds.

Remove them with a draining spoon and you should find that the skins slip off easily. Now place the skinned peach halves in the vinegar and sugar mixture, bring it up to simmering point and gently poach the fruit for 15 minutes or until tender when tested with a skewer. Use a draining spoon to remove the peaches and transfer them to the warmed preserving jar. Boil the syrup rapidly to reduce it to approximately half its volume, then pour through a strainer over the peaches.

Seal the jar and keep for 6 weeks before using.

PORK

Roast Loin of Pork

Serves 6-8
Prep time: 15 mins
Cook time: 2 hours and 5 mins

1.8kg loin of pork, on the bone
1 tablespoon sunflower oil
Sea salt
Plenty of freshly milled black
  pepper

This can be served hot, or is equally delicious served cold and thinly sliced.

Preheat the oven to its maximum temperature. Rub the crackling with the oil, and sprinkle with salt and pepper. Lay it on a rack in a roasting pan, and if there are bone ends cover these with foil.

Roast for 15 minutes in the very hot oven, then turn down to 190 C/370 F and cook for 1 hour and 50 minutes, basting occasionally. When it's done, if serving the pork hot, remove the bone with a small knife, then remove the crackling in one piece and discard the fat between the meat and crackling. Carve into thin slices, and break the crackling into thin strips alongside it on a large serving platter. Reserve the juices for gravy.

If serving cold, allow to cool and place in the refrigerator for the next day and remove the bone and crackling as above.

Pulled Pork

Serves 12
Prep time: 15 mins
Cook time: 4-8 hours

2.5kg boneless shoulder of pork
2 tsp smoked paprika
2tsp ground cumin
2 tsp black pepper
2 tsp brown sugar
1 tsp salt
750ml/ 3 cups dry apple cider
375ml/ 1½ cups smoky barbecue sauce

Mix together 2 tsp each smoked paprika, ground cumin, pepper, and brown sugar, plus 1 tsp salt. Rub over the 2.5kg boneless shoulder of pork. Put the pork in a big casserole dish, skin-side up, and pour in the cider. Cover with a lid and cook in the oven at 150C/130C fan/gas 2 for anywhere between 4 and 8 hrs until falling apart. Check every few hours in case it gets dry – if it does, add more cider.

Take it out of the oven and put the meat in a big dish, leaving the liquid in the casserole. Cut the skin off, then shred the meat using two forks. Ditch any fatty bits, and skim any excess fat off the surface of the sauce. Add about half the smoky BBQ sauce to the casserole, mix it in, then ladle some into a bowl for dipping.

Put the pulled pork back in the casserole with the juices so it stays moist. Season to taste. *Can be made one day ahead.*

Barbecue Spare Ribs

Serves 4-6
Prep time: 20 mins
Cook time: 1 hour 45 mins

2 racks pork loin back ribs
  (about 1.6kg)

MARINADE:
1 fresh red chilli
1 thumb size piece fresh ginger
2 cloves garlic
150ml unsweetened apple juice
100ml white wine vinegar
2 heaped tablespoons tomato
  ketchup
1 tablespoon Dijon mustard
100ml dark soy sauce
100g soft dark brown sugar

Preheat the oven to 200°C/gas 6 or fire up your barbecue.

Drizzle a little oil over the ribs, season with sea salt and black pepper and rub all over to coat, then make the marinade. Deseed and finely chop the chilli, peel and grate the ginger and garlic then place them all in a medium pan along with the apple juice, white wine vinegar, tomato ketchup, mustard, soy sauce and brown sugar. Whisk the ingredients together and place the pan over a medium heat. Stir until the sugar dissolves, then simmer for 10 to 15 minutes, or until the sauce has thickened.

Cook in the oven for 75 minutes, basting occasionally, removing the foil for the final 15 minutes. Either transfer to the barbecue for 10 minutes grilling, or turn on the broiler in the oven to blacken them slightly. Transfer to a board and carve.

Slow Braised Pig's Cheeks

Serves 4-6
Prep time: 45 mins
Cook time: 3 hours

3 tbsp plain (all purpose) flour
1 tsp paprika
1kg trimmed pigs cheeks (10-12),
  cut in half if very thick
3 tbsp olive oil
1 onion roughly chopped
3 celery sticks roughly chopped
2 carrots roughly chopped
2 garlic cloves roughly chopped
2 tbsp tomato puree
200ml red wine
500ml beef stock
1 bouquet garni
1 small bunch fresh sage,
  roughly chopped

Heat the oven to 160°C/140°C fan/320 F/gas 3. Mix the flour with the paprika and plenty of salt and pepper in a shallow bowl, then roll the pig cheeks in the mixture to coat.

Heat 2 tbsp oil in the casserole and fry the cheeks in batches until browned all over. Set aside, then add the remaining oil to the pan and add the onion. Cook gently, colouring as little as possible, for 5 minutes. Add the celery and carrots and fry for 5 minutes more, stirring often. Add the garlic and tomato purée and cook for a minute or two before returning the cheeks to the pan. Pour in the red wine and simmer for a few minutes, scraping the brown bits from the bottom of the pan.

Cover the pork and vegetables with the stock, then tie the thyme, rosemary, parsley, sage sprig and bay leaves together with string and add to the casserole. Cover with the lid and transfer to the oven. Cook for about 3 hours or until the pig cheeks are tender and come apart easily.

Venison Stew

Serves: 12
Prep time: 30 mins
Cook time: 2 hours

2kg/ 4lbs diced venison
450g/ 1lb fat salt pork
(or pork belly)
1 pig's trotter (optional)
450g/ 1lb onions, peeled
and chopped
450g/ 1lb carrots cut into
rounds
1 dessertspoon dark muscovado
sugar
1 tsp thyme chopped
1 tsp juniper berries
575ml/ 2 cups beef stock
275ml/ 1 ¼ cups Guinness
or dark stout
Oil for frying
Salt and pepper

Preheat the oven to 150 C/300 F.

Brown the onions and carrots in some oil then transfer to a casserole. Sauté the diced salt pork and finally the venison. Add to the vegetables, season with salt and pepper and pour in the stock and Guinness. Lay the pig's trotter on top (if using), cover and cook for 2 hours or until the meat is tender. Remove the trotter, blot off any excess fat from the casserole surface with kitchen paper then thicken with Beurre Manié (see below).

Beurre Manié

Melt 30g/2 tablespoons butter in a pan, and add a large tablespoon plain flour. Mix together and drop bits at a time whisking into the casserole. This will thicken the gravy.

Mustard Suprême of Rabbit

Serves: 4-6
Prep time: 10 mins
Cook time: 30 mins

1 rabbit, jointed
10 sprigs fresh thyme
1 large clove garlic
500ml/ 2 cups chicken stock
1 tbsp peppercorns
1 bay leaf
15g/ 1 tbsp butter

FOR THE SAUCE
15g/ 1tbsp butter
15g/ 1tsbp plain flour
Broth from the rabbit casserole above
1 tbsp English mustard
Fresh parsley
100ml/ ½ cup double/heavy cream
Salt and pepper

Add the stock, bay leaf, peppercorns, garlic and thyme to a large stockpot then add the rabbit joints. Cover the pan with a lid and simmer on the hob over a low heat - 45 minutes to an hour. Pierce the meat to check when tender, and when ready, remove from heat, strain and reserve the broth. Set meat and broth aside.

Add the butter to a medium saucepan, and melt over a low heat. Add the flour, stirring with hand whisk. Then add the rabbit stock bit by bit, stirring continuously, until the sauce is thick and smooth. Add the double cream and bring to the boil. Remove from the heat and add parsley, mustard and seasoning to taste.

Finally take a frying pan, melt the remaining 15g butter and add the thyme sprigs. Cook for a minute then add the rabbit pieces and fry until golden brown. Remove from the pan to a serving dish and pour the sauce over the rabbit, garnishing with any leftover parsley and thyme leaves.

Pheasant Fricassée

Serves: 4
Prep time: 15 mins
Cook time: 1 hour

4 pheasant breasts
40g/ 3 tbsp butter
1 onion, chopped
3 leeks, chopped
1 clove garlic, crushed
220g/8oz mushrooms, sliced
60ml/ ¼ cup brandy
1tbsp plain flour
1litre/ 4 cups chicken stock
1tbsp fresh thyme
2 tbsp fresh chopped parsley
1 bay leaf
220ml/ 1 cup double/heavy cream

Poach pheasant breasts in boiling water seasoned with a few pieces of onion, garlic, bay leaves and some salt and pepper for approx. 10 minutes.

Heat butter in a heavy casserole or dutch oven and add chopped onion and leeks. Cook for 5-10 minutes until translucent and just starting to brown lightly. Add mushrooms and cook until tender, add the brandy and let it reduce.

Sprinkle the mixture with flour to coat all ingredients, add stock and herbs. Simmer the mixture for about 10 minutes, then remove from the heat and add cream. Shred the cooked and cooled pheasant and stir into the mixture.

Fried Quail with Onions

Serves: 2 as a main , 4 as a first
Prep time: 15 mins
Cook time: 1 hour

4 quails
5 tbsp olive oil
2 large onions, peeled, halved
  and sliced
125ml/ ½ cup brandy
4 large slices firm white bread,
  crusts removed and fried in oil
  or toasted

Pull off any remaining feathers or singe them off over a flame, then rinse the quails and pat them dry with kitchen paper. Heat the oil in a wide, heavy frying pan or casserole and put in the onions. Cover and cook slowly over a very low heat for about 30 minutes until they are very soft and beginning to colour, stirring often.

Push the onions to one side, put the quails into the pan and season with salt and pepper. Turn up the heat to medium. Keep turning the quails to brown them all over — around 7 or 8 minutes — and stir the onions so that they brown evenly. Add the brandy and cook, covered, over a low heat for 25 to 30 minutes until the onions are caramelized and the quails are done. Pull the leg of one of the quails — if it moves easily they are cooked. They should still be a little pink. Serve them on toasted or fried sliced bread.

Game Pie

Serves: 6–8
Prep time: 1-2 hours
Cooking time: 2-3 hours

You will need a French raised game pie tin

PIE INGREDIENTS

1 tbsp butter
1 onion fine chopped
2 cloves of garlic grated
2 pheasant breasts
4 pigeon breasts
250g/ 2 cups diced rabbit
250g/ 2 cups diced venison
2 sprigs of thyme
1 sage leaf
1 small pinch of mace
1 egg beaten
Salt
White and black pepper
300ml/ 1 ¼ cups game or beef stock
Gelatin leaves

FOR THE PATE

1 shallot finely diced
1 garlic clove grated
A knob of butter
Dash of oil
500g/ 4 cups trimmed chicken livers
1 sprig of thyme
1 small pinch of mace
Salt
Black pepper
150ml/ ½ cup brandy
50ml/ ¼ cup double/heavy cream

HOT WATER CRUST

110g/ ½ cup lard
110g/ ½ cup butter
200ml/ ¾ cup water
2 eggs beaten
10g salt
550g/ 3 ½ cups plain flour

Preheat the oven to 180 C/ 356 F

THE HOT WATER CRUST

Make the hot water crust first. Place the butter, lard and water in a saucepan and bring to a boil, then take off the heat. Meanwhile in a large bowl place the flour and salt, pour in the beaten eggs, mix and then the hot fat. With a spoon or hands mix the two together to form a ball and leave on the side covered with some baking paper.

THE PATÉ

In a frying pan soften the shallots and garlic in the butter and oil, add the chicken livers and thyme, sear until almost cooked. Add the brandy, seasoning and mace, cook for 1 minute. Place in a blender and pulse until smooth, add a little cream for a richer paté, taste and season again if needed. Place in an airtight container in the fridge while assembling the pie.

LINING THE TIN WITH PASTRY

Take two thirds of the pastry, pull off a tennis ball size piece and work it by hand over the bottom and up the sides of the tin. Add more and work until all sides are covered. Roll out the remaining one third to fit the size of the pie lid.

FILLING THE PIE

Season all the game with salt and black pepper, tightly layer the pheasant in the bottom of the pie followed by the paté, next the diced venison and rabbit and lastly the pigeon. Egg wash the rim and place on the pastry lid, cut a small hole in the centre of the pie lid.

Cook in the oven for 30 minutes, then turn the oven down to 150 C/300 F and cook for a further 1 hour 20 minutes. Remove from the oven and leave to stand for 10 minutes, gently remove the clips and the sides from the tin, egg wash the whole pie and put back in the oven for 10-15 minutes to set the glaze and firm up the sides. Remove from oven and leave to cool.

THE JELLY

Soak the gelatin leaves in cold water, place in a pan with the stock and bring to a simmer, stir until the gelatin is dissolved. Remove from the heat and pour into a jug, leave to cool. Using a small funnel or syringe fill the pie cavity until some of the jelly reaches the top. Chill in the fridge for at least 4 hours until the jelly is set.

Fried Chicken with Gravy

Serves: 6-8
Prep time: 2 hours
Cook time: 1 hour

2 chickens, jointed into
  6 pieces each
500g lard (shortening)
100g plain flour
500ml/ 1 pint double/heavy cream
½ tsp mace
Salt & pepper to taste

Put all the chicken joints into a large pan of water and leave for about 2 hours – this will tenderize the meat. Drain the chicken, pat dry and drop into a bowl full of the flour, seasoned well with salt and pepper. Flour the joints all over.

In a frying pan, melt all the lard so that it fills the pan halfway. Drop about half the chicken pieces into the pan and fry on each side. Take these out and keep warm in a hot dish in the oven. Fry the rest of the chicken. When done, pour the fat out of the pan and place back on the stove. Pour in the pint of cream, a tablespoon of the seasoned flour, pepper, salt and the mace. Heat slowly and whisk through, and this should thicken slightly to a nice gravy. Pour over the chicken and serve.

Chicken Hash

Serves: 4
Prep time: 45 mins
Cook time: 45 mins

4 chicken breasts (or leftover
  cooked chicken enough for 4)
4 medium size potatoes, peeled,
  boiled and cut into small squares.
500ml/ 4 cups chicken stock
30g/ 1 heaped tbsp flour
30g/ 1 heaped tbsp butter
100ml double/heavy cream
½ wineglass of sherry
1 tbsp chopped parsley
Salt & pepper to taste

Poach the chicken breasts in the chicken stock until tender. Drain, reserving the stock, and let the chicken cool. When cool, shred finely or chop into small squares.

In a frying pan, melt the butter and mix in the flour to form a roux. Cook for a minute, then slowly add in the reserved stock, about 200-300ml to make a sauce. Add the cream, sherry, salt and pepper, check seasoning, then add in the chopped chicken and potatoes. Scatter with the chopped parsley and serve.

Poulet Crapaudine (with Onions and Prunes)

Serves: 4
Prep time: 45 mins
Cook time: 1 hour

1 whole fresh chicken
1 lemon
12 button onions, peeled
12 prunes either tinned
  or soaked in water, stoned
2 tbsp caster/superfine sugar
2 tbsp red wine vinegar
Salt and pepper
Butter

Preheat oven to 220 C / 428 F

Prepare the chicken by spreading butter over it. Squeeze the lemon juice over the chicken, and stuff the cavity with the lemon halves. Season and put in the oven at 220 C/428 F heat for 20 minutes then reduce the oven to 180 C/355 F for 40-50 minutes. Baste at least twice during this time. It's cooked when a knife inserted between the leg and the breast shows the juice running clear.

Melt some more butter in a saucepan and add the peeled onions. Season well, then cover with and cook on a low heat for 30 minutes until soft. Heat the prunes in a second saucepan and keep warm. In a third saucepan, dissolve the caster sugar slowly then add the vinegar and reduce by a third. Decant the onions and prunes into two separate sauceboats, and divide the sauce between them. Hand round with the roast chicken.

Devilled Turkey

Serves: 4
Prep time: 15 mins
Cook time: 40 mins

4 turkey legs, 4 turkey wings
  (you can use chicken as well)
2 tsp English mustard
1 tsp cayenne pepper
1 tsp salt
200g/ 1 ½ cups cranberry sauce
2 tbsp Worcestershire sauce
2 tbsp walnut ketchup
  (mushroom ketchup is also good)
2 tbsp soft brown sugar
1 tbsp red wine vinegar

Preheat oven grill to high.

Make 2 or 3 deep incisions in the turkey pieces with a sharp knife and rub the mustard, cayenne pepper and salt all over them. Place in a baking tray lined with foil and grill each side until brown. While this is happening, mix the remaining ingredients in an oven proof baking dish.

Remove the turkey from the grill, and switch the oven on to 180 C/ 355 F. Place the turkey pieces into the oven dish with the sauce mixture. Baste and bake in the oven for 20-30 minutes, basting every 10 minutes, until tender.

Chicken Gumbo

Serves: A crowd!
Prep time: 1½ hours
Cooking time: 4 hours

1 whole chicken (about 4 pounds)

1⅓ cups (165g) vegetable oil

1⅓ cups (165g) all-purpose flour

1 green bell pepper diced

1 bunch diced celery

4 onions diced

1 head of garlic, peeled and minced
(about 8 to 10 cloves)

3 (28oz/ 400g) tins of tomatoes,
crushed or diced

1 ½ cups/ 240g Andouille
sausage, sliced and quartered,
Chorizo makes a good substitute
if Andouille can't be sourced.

4 to 6 bay leaves

1 tablespoon Tabasco sauce

1 tablespoon sea salt, plus more
to taste

2 teaspoons freshly ground
black pepper, plus more to taste

Cayenne pepper, to taste

Thinly sliced flat leaf parsley to
garnish

Place chicken in a large pot and cover with water. Add leftover onion and celery trimmings if desired. Salt lightly. Bring to a boil, then reduce to a gentle simmer, removing any foam as necessary. Cook approximately 45 minutes to an hour, turning occasionally, or until chicken is cooked through. Remove chicken and allow to cool, reserving broth. Shred once cool. Add the leftover bones back to the stock and continue simmering until ready to use.

To make roux, heat the oil in a large soup pot at medium heat until shimmery, about 2 minutes. Add the flour and whisk until blended. Continue whisking constantly until desired color is reached. A caramel colour takes a minimum of 25 minutes. You can go until you reach a coffee colour, about 40 minutes.

Keeping heat at medium, add peppers, celery, onions, and garlic to the roux and cook until tender, about 5 - 8 minutes. Add the shredded chicken, tomatoes with their juices, sausage, bay leaves, Tabasco, salt, pepper, and cayenne. Pour in the chicken stock (reserved from earlier), plus additional stock or water if needed to cover. Bring mixture to a boil, then reduce heat to a gentle simmer. Cook for at least 4 hours or longer. Adjust seasonings to taste. (If you have time, cool and reheat the next day, when it tastes even better.)

Serve gumbo with additional hot sauce and cooked white rice.

Lobster Newburg

Serves: 4
Prep time: 10 mins
Cook time: 10 mins

1kg/ 2 ¼ cups rock lobster tail

300ml/ 1 ¼ cups vegetable or
  fish stock of which 50% is
  white wine

75g/5 tbsp unsalted butter

6 tbsp brandy

12 tbsp Madeira or sherry

170g/ ⅔ cup double/heavy cream

Salt and pepper

2 egg yolks

1 tbsp single cream

Remove lobster meat from the tail shell and cut into half inch medallions. Simmer the stock for 5 minutes, then add the lobster. Simmer for 3 minutes only – do not cook it through.

Meanwhile, melt butter in a frying pan. Remove the lobster, drain and transfer into the melted butter.

Warm the brandy in a third pan and set alight. Pour the flaming brandy into the frying pan, gently stirring. Add the Madeira or sherry, swirl once then add the double cream. Turn heat up slightly and reduce sauce a little. Finally beat the egg yolks and add to pan together with the single cream. Mix in to thicken sauce. Season and serve.

Fishcakes

Serves: 4
Prep time: 30 mins plus chilling time
Cook time: 20 mins

225g/ 1 ¼ cups cooked fish: cod,
  haddock and salmon, skin and
  boneless

220g/ ½ cup mashed potato
  (no milk or butter added)

15g/ 2 tbsp butter at room temperature

2 tbsp chopped parsley

Salt and pepper

1 egg beaten

White breadcrumbs

Sunflower oil for frying

In a large bowl mix the fish with the mashed potato, beat in the butter, chopped parsley, salt & pepper and blend until smooth. Chill in the fridge for at least 2-4 hours. Then form into round cakes on a floured board. Dip into the beaten egg, then into the breadcrumbs and fry in sunflower oil until golden on both sides. Makes 4 large fishcakes.

Sole Colbert

Serves: 4
Prep time: 30 mins
Cook time: 10 mins

1 x 400g/ ½ lb Dover sole (or Lemon
   Sole) per person, skinned and
   without the head
30g/ 3 tbsp plain flour seasoned
   with salt and pepper
1 egg, beaten
50g/ 1 cup white breadcrumbs
   sunflower oil

PARSLEY BUTTER
15g butter
1 tsp chopped parsley
1 lemon
½ tsp lemon juice

Make the parsley butter first: soften the butter in a bowl. Grate in the zest from half the lemon, add the parsley and lemon juice. Mix well, then form butter into a roll in paper or foil and chill until firm.

Make an incision down the centre of the thick side of the fish, between the two fillets and cut through a section of the backbone, about 5cm long. Dip in the flour, then the egg and then the breadcrumbs. Fry till golden brown in sunflower oil, then part the fillets where they have been cut and remove the bone. Serve immediately with a slice of the parsley butter on top.

Lady Stanley's 'Kedgerie of Salmon'

Serves: 4-6
Prep time: 15 mins
Cook time: 25 mins

300g/ 1 ⅓ cups basmati rice
100g/ ⅓ cup unsalted butter
1 small red onion, finely chopped
225g/ 1 ¼ cups cooked smoked
   salmon, cut into chunks or flaked
4 hard boiled eggs
4 spring onions/scallions,
   finely shredded
Juice of 1 lime
Small bunch dill, finely chopped

Put the rice into a large heavy-based saucepan, pour over 700ml/1¼ pints water and sprinkle in a good shake of salt. Cover and bring to the boil, then remove the lid and allow all the water to be absorbed – this should take about 15 minutes. Turn off the heat, cover again and allow to steam dry.

Melt half the butter with the oil in a large frying pan. Add the onion and cook until softened and beginning to brown. Add the rice and quickly stir to make sure all the buttery juices are absorbed and the rice is heated through. Mix in the salmon, eggs, spring onions, lime juice and dill. Stir gently, along with cubes of the remaining butter and serve.

Cliveden Baked Haddock Fillets

Serves: 4–5
Prep time: 10 mins
Cooking time: 15 mins

1kg/ 2.2lbs haddock fillet, skin and
   bones removed and sliced into
   5 even sized portions
5 field mushrooms, sliced thinly
25g/ 2 tbsp unsalted butter, softened
Olive oil
300ml/ 2 ¼ cups double/heavy cream
Sea salt
Cayenne pepper
Small bunch chopped chives

Preheat the oven grill.

Take an ovenproof dish large enough to accommodate all the ingredients comfortably, and brush with the softened butter. Then add the haddock portions and season lightly with salt and pepper.

Gently fry the sliced mushrooms in a frying pan with olive oil until golden. You will need to do this in batches, so the pan is not too full. Season each batch with sea salt as you cook and transfer onto a kitchen paper lined oven tray when cooked.

Once all mushrooms are cooked, scatter over the fish, pour over the double cream then grill under the preheated grill until golden and bubbling.

Sprinkle with cayenne pepper to taste and the chopped chives then serve immediately, with some fine green beans or asparagus.

(This would also make a good lunch dish, served with a green salad and some crusty bread).

CHAPTER 3

NANCY LANCASTER

'Two years after my first husband Henry Field died, I married his cousin Ronald Tree. I went into a shop to change my address and said, "I used to be Mrs Field, now I'm Mrs Tree." All the man said to me was "You're very rural."'

VEGETABLES & SALADS

'Dearest Alice,' wrote Nancy Astor to her niece Alice Winn in 1939, 'I know the children will have told you all about the party, and Joyce [Grenfell] says that she is going to write. It really was a grand affair. Anne looked after Princess Elizabeth and Elizabeth after Margaret Rose. Here is a picture of them both. It was a strenuous day for me, especially as we had three Queens. Queen Mary arrived as the clock struck four...certainly no one had a better time than she did. She served at a stall, sucked ice-cream cornets, laughed heartily at the conjuror, and applauded him loudly.'

Nancy's historic election in 1919 allowed her to entertain not just as a prominent hostess but as a Parliamentarian in her own right. This gave her the edge on her society compatriots – Ettie Desborough, Jennie Churchill and May Goelet, then the Duchess of Roxburghe – who had relied on their feminine charms and (and sometimes lovers) to secure their social circle. Nancy Astor never exploited her beauty in such ways. Years later, when Nancy Lancaster aged 80, was asked by a television interviewer about the sex life between her aunt and Lord Astor, remarked without blinking, "they didn't have sex, they had children." Nancy Astor was confident, fearless, sometimes tactless, a serious person interested in people and in causes; a seductress she was not. "Stop squeelin'" she would shout down the dining table, "You're talkin' like a lunatic."

The Mirador recipe book came into its own as menus were cut down to four or five courses. The American preference for lighter food, with an array of vegetables imaginatively cooked and the introduction of chopped and fresh salads absolutely revolutionised the way English meals were constructed.

The recipes in this chapter reveal a diet constructed for people who enjoyed a wholesome, outdoor way of life, and taking strenuous exercise was another accomplishment that the American heiresses brought with them. Nancy was no exception. Slim and fit her entire life, she rode and hunted, swam every day in the Thames when at Cliveden, or skated on it when it froze in winter. She played tennis, squash and golf to almost professional standards, acquiring a house, Rest Harrow at Sandwich, to further improve her handicap. Banished for eternity now, the Edwardian hostesses of the past could only look on as fashion changed and corsets were abandoned. Eating well and healthily was the only way to maintain a figure suited to the short, sleek dresses of the Roaring Twenties and Thirties. Food had to keep up with the trend.

New vegetables were grown and cooked, such as aubergines (eggplant), salsify, Jerusalem artichokes (sunchokes) and sweet potatoes, or rather hardly new to English kitchen gardens but much neglected. As many as four or five vegetable dishes, each cooked separately, with a simple meat dish, like roast chicken or grilled lamb cutlets, were given. 'The composite salad, in which lettuce, fruit finely cut up, and sliced nuts are delicately mixed with some variety of mayonnaise, hollandaise or tartare sauce, and put in the same bowl as the straw sliced chicken, tongue, ham or shredded lobster or prawn' said Vogue in 1927, 'are a good deal served.' Many of these can be found in the Mirador cookbook – for example, Cobb, Waldorf and Pullman – together with exotic salad dressings. Lord Astor's recipe emerges from this period on p82, while dressings made from sour cream, onion juice and paprika or fresh lemon juice, mustard and caraway seeds added flavour and zest to dishes that were a meal in themselves. By the time that Nancy Astor's niece, Nancy Tree (as she then was) arrived in England in 1926, mealtimes at Cliveden and St James's Square – and at other fashionable London hostesses' – had already despatched the cumbersome eight course Edwardian menus into the distant past.

OPPOSITE: Nancy Astor drives off at Walton Heath Golf Club watched by fellow MP for Harborough, Lord Castle Stewart, July 1931

Corn Fritters

Makes 12
Prep time: less than 30 mins
Cook time: 10-30 mins

300g/ 10.5oz sweetcorn (either
   from a can, or freshly cooked)
3 spring onions/scallions,
   very finely chopped chopped
3 free-range eggs
30ml/ 1fl oz milk
75g/ 2½oz plain flour
½ tsp cayenne pepper
Vegetable oil, for frying
Salt and freshly ground black pepper

To make the fritters, put the sweetcorn and spring onions in a bowl. Beat the eggs with the milk. Pour this mixture over the sweetcorn and mix well. Season with salt and pepper. Sieve the flour with the cayenne pepper and then stir into the sweetcorn mixture.

Add the oil to a large frying pan – you need to shallow fry these, so make sure the base of the pan is well covered. (CAUTION: hot oil can be dangerous. Do not leave unattended.) Heat the oil then test by adding a tiny bit of the batter – it should immediately start bubbling around the edges when it hits the oil. Using a small ladle, drop batter onto the oil – you need around 2 tbsp of mixture per fritter. You should be able to fry 4–5 at any one time. Fry for a couple of minutes on one side until light brown then turn over and cook for a further minute.

Turn out onto kitchen paper to remove any excess oil and keep warm in a low oven. Continue until you have used all the batter.

Corn Pudding

Serves: 2-3
Prep time: 10 mins
Cook time: 10-15 mins

340g/ 2 cups frozen
  (but defrosted) or 1 tin
  sweetcorn
1 egg
3 tbsp double/heavy cream
  (depending on the number of
  people)
½ tsp grated or ground nutmeg

Preheat the oven to 200 C/390 F. Grease a small soufflé dish.

Beat the egg and cream together well. Add a pinch of salt, the nutmeg and the sweetcorn. Mix again, then put into the soufflé dish. Put the soufflé dish into a baking tray and fill with water halfway up the dish. Put in the oven for about 10-15 minutes until the top is brown.

Cornmeal Soufflé Grits

Serves: 4
Prep time: 30 mins
Cook time: 20 mins

260g/ 1cup grits
250ml/ 1 cup milk
125ml/ ½ cup double/heavy cream
2 eggs
Salt to taste

Preheat the oven to 200 C/390 F. Grease an ovenproof baking dish.

Boil 250ml/1 cup water and add the grits, whisking all the time until thickened. (The mixture needs to be thick for this recipe). Once all the water has absorbed, leave in the pan to cool. When cool, whisk in the eggs, cream and salt. Transfer to the baking dish and cook in a hot oven for 20-30 minutes until risen and brown.

Potatoes Dauphinoise

Serves: 4
Prep time: 45 mins
Cook time: 1 hr

1kg/ 2lb 4oz floury potatoes
   such as Yukon Gold, Idaho Russet,
   King Edward or Maris Piper sliced
   into thin rounds, about 3mm thick.
3-4 garlic cloves, finely chopped
500ml/2 cups double/heavy cream
Salt and black pepper to taste

Preheat the oven to 160 C/ 320 F. Grease an ovenproof gratin dish.

Place the potato slices and grated garlic in a bowl and season to taste. Pour over the cream and mix well. Pour into a large gratin dish.

Press the potato down with the back of a spoon or your hands so it forms a solid layer. The cream should come to just below the top layer of potato, top up with more double cream if necessary.

Bake for 1-1½ hours, or until the potatoes are completely tender.

Les Pommes Rissolées

Serves: 4-6
Prep time: 15 mins
Cook time: 20 mins

680g/ 1 ½ lb new potatoes,
   scraped or peeled
75g/ ⅓ cup butter

Cook the scraped potatoes in boiling, lightly salted water. Remove the pan at once, and drain the potatoes.

Melt the butter in a heavy based frying pan/skillet, and cook the potatoes, covered, until golden.

Pommes D'Anna

Serves: 6
Prep time:25 mins
Cook time: 2 hours

125g/ ½ cup duck fat

3 garlic cloves, unpeeled but
 lightly crushed with the flat
 of a knife

3-4 fresh thyme sprigs, plus
 3 extra thyme sprigs, leaves
 picked

2 bay leaves

1.25kg/ 2 ½ lbs Yukon Gold,
 Idaho Russet, King Edward or
 Maris Piper potatoes

Put the duck fat in a pan with the garlic, whole thyme sprigs and bay leaves. Heat gently for 5-10 minutes to melt the fat, then set aside to infuse for 20 minutes – somewhere warm so the fat doesn't solidify. Remove and discard the aromatics.

Meanwhile, peel the potatoes and slice very thinly (a mandoline is best for this). Wash the slices in cold water to remove any excess starch, then pat dry on kitchen paper.

Heat the oven to 200°C/fan180°C/gas 6. Put the potato slices in a bowl and toss with the infused fat. Warm a 20cm non-stick, ovenproof frying pan over a low heat. Layer up the slices of potato in overlapping circles in the pan, seasoning every so often and sprinkling with some of the extra thyme leaves, until all the potatoes are used up. Continue to cook over a very low heat for 10-15 minutes ?to help the potatoes crisp up and brown. Shake the pan gently every so often to prevent the potato slices catching and burning.

Cover with a sheet of baking paper and a lid (or foil), transfer to the oven and bake for 45-55 minutes until tender to the point of a knife. Cool for 10 minutes. Turn out onto a board or serving plate, then serve in wedges.

Stuffed Aubergine

Serves: 2-4
Prep time: 30 mins
Cook time: 30 mins

1 large aubergine
30g/ 1 tbsp butter
60g/ ½ cup breadcumbs
125ml/ ½ cup single (thin)
 cream

Preheat the oven to 180 C/ 355 F. Grease a baking tray.

Cut off the stem of the aubergine and slice vertically in two. Scoop out the flesh inside, slice and add to boiling water. Parboil until easily mashed like potato. Then add breadcrumbs, butter, cream, salt and pepper. Put back into both shells and bake in the oven for half an hour. Serve in the shells.

Mrs Gibson's Carrots

Serves: 2-4
Prep time: 30 mins
Cook time: 30 mins

6 large carrots (about 600g)
30g brown sugar
30g butter
Salt and pepper to taste

Preheat the oven to 180 C/ 355 F. Grease a medium oven dish.

Peel and slice the carrots into sticks, then parboil in boiling water until tender. Place in layers in the oven dish, putting a sprinkle of brown sugar, dots of butter and a little salt and pepper between each layer and on the top. Fill the dish with warm water, place in the oven and bake for about 20 minutes until brown, and the syrup has thickened. Serve in the oven dish.

Broad Beans with Artichokes

Serves: 4
Prep time: 1 hour
Cook time: 20 mins

450g/ 3 ¾ cups shelled broad/
  fava beans
3 artichokes
30g/ 2 tbsp butter
150ml/ ¾ cup chicken, veal
  or vegetable stock
Salt and pepper
1 ½ tbsp chopped chervil

Cook the beans and the artichokes separately in salted water. The beans should take about 20 minutes and the artichokes longer – around 45 minutes. Drain both and then discard the leaves and choke from the artichokes.

Cut up the artichoke hearts into small dice. Melt 30g of the butter in a saucepan. Add the beans, cook for a minute, then add the stock, salt and pepper. Simmer for 10 minutes, covered. Turn into a serving dish and sprinkle over the chervil.

Gratin of Salsify

Serves: 4-6
Prep time: 45 mins
Cook time: 20 mins

500g/ 10 cups salsify roots,
  cleaned and peeled
60g/ 2 tbsp butter
60g/ 2 tbsp plain flour
500ml/2 cups whole milk
1 tsp ground or grated nutmeg
Salt and pepper to taste

Preheat the oven to 180 C/ 355 F. Grease a medium oven dish.

Peel and cut the salsify roots into small chunks. Cook in lightly salted, boiling water for about 45 minutes. While this is happening, make the béchamel sauce. In a small saucepan, melt the butter then add the flour. Mix together and cook for a few seconds before slowly adding the milk, whisking all the time to prevent lumps. When the sauce is ready, add the nutmeg, salt and pepper.

When tender, drain the salsify and put into the oven dish. Pour over the sauce, dot with a few bits of butter and put into the oven to brown on the top.

Creamed Celery

Serves: 4
Prep time: 20 mins
Cook time: 20 mins

1 bunch fresh celery
300ml/ 1 cup single cream
30g/ 1 tbsp butter
Salt and pepper to taste

Clean and remove any strings from the celery, then dice. Put into boiling salted water and cook for 15 minutes. Drain, place in a serving dish and keep warm.

While the celery is cooking, heat the cream and butter together until just boiling. Add salt and pepper and pour over the celery. Serve immediately or keep warm in the oven until needed.

Asparagus with a Hollandaise Mousseline Sauce

Serves: 2-4
Prep time: 30 mins
Cook time: 30 mins

24 asparagus (6 per person or
  more if preferred)

HOLLANDAISE
MOUSSELINE SAUCE:
4 egg yolks
A pinch of sea salt
180g/ ¾ cup unsalted butter
1 ½ tbsp lemon juice
4 tbsp double/heavy or whipping
  cream

See p31 Eggs Benedict recipe for the hollandaise. To transform this into a mousseline, fold in whipped cream before serving.

To cook the asparagus, trim the woody ends by bending the stalks to find the natural break point, and snapping them off . Bring a pan of salted water to the boil and cook for no more than 4-5 minutes. Drain and arrange on a serving dish, hand the hollandaise round in a sauceboat or add a spoonful per plate.

Braised Turnips with Spinach

Seves: 4-6
Prep time: 15 mins
Cook time: 15 mins

450g/ 1 lb turnips
1 tbsp olive oil
1 tbsp butter
1 spring lemon thyme (or thyme)
2 tbsp spring onions/scallions,
    finely chopped
200g/ 1 cup fresh spinach
Salt and pepper

Peel the turnips and cut in quarters, or sixths if large. Place a large frying pan on a medium heat and add the olive oil. Add the turnips when the oil is hot.

Cook until turnips are brown on one side, then turn over and add the spring onions and thyme to the pan. When turnips are tender, add the spinach and butter, and cook until spinach has wilted. Season with salt and pepper.

Cabbage the Haseley Way

Serves: 4-6
Prep time: 20 mins
Cook ime: 20 mins

1 young cabbage
3 tbsp melted butter
1 tbsp hot sauce
A pinch of sugar
A pinch of bicarbonate of soda
Salt and pepper

Cut the cabbage in half and put into quickly boiling salted water for 5 minutes with the bicarbonate of soda. Drain and put back into the saucepan. Now pour over fresh boiling water so the cabbage is almost covered, with a little salt and a little sugar. Cook with the lid off until tender.

Drain the cabbage and shred it finely. Just before serving, pour over some melted butter and the hot sauce, with another sprinkling of salt and pepper.

Stewed Creole Tomatoes

Serves: 6
Prep time: 1½ hours
Cooking time: 2 hours

3 ripe medium-large Creole/Beef
  or other large ripe tomatoes
1 tablespoon olive oil
1 large white onion, quartered
  and cut into slices
1-14.5 oz/ 400g tin chopped
  tomatoes with juice
1 stalk celery with leaves, diced
2 tablespoons fresh parsley,
  chopped
2 teaspoons Worcestershire sauce
1 tablespoon sugar (or more if you
  like sweet stewed tomatoes)
1 teaspoon fresh basil
½ teaspoon salt
½ teaspoon garlic powder or
  1 clove fresh garlic, crushed
Black pepper to taste
2 tablespoons melted butter
125g/ ½ cup breadcrumbs

The way these were traditionally cooked at Mirador was to stew down for hours and then bottle the 'sugo' (which it essentially was, but without the addition of garlic or olive oil). This version is a combination with fresh tomatoes, and baked in the oven. It is a perfect vegan dish, if you substitute the buttered breadcrumbs with olive oil.

Pre-heat oven to 180 c/350 F degrees. Grease a 9 x 9inch oven dish

To blanch and peel tomatoes, first run a sharp knife around the circumference of each tomato, just piercing the skin, then boil a kettle and pour the hot water into a large bowl. Add the tomatoes. Occasionally turn them to make sure all sides of tomatoes are submerged. After about 20 minutes run cold water into the bowl. When cool enough to handle, remove skins — they should slide off. Set tomatoes aside.

Add oil to a frying pan and heat to medium high. Add onion slices, stir and sauté for about 5 minutes until onions begin to turn translucent. Remove from heat and set aside.

Add the tinned tomatoes, sauteed onions, celery, fresh parsley to the dish and stir.

Add Worcestershire sauce, sugar, dried basil, salt, garlic and black pepper and stir to combine.

Remove the cores of blanched, peeled tomatoes. Cut the tomatoes in eighths. Add and stir to .

Cover tightly with aluminum foil. Bake in the oven for 1 hour.

Remove the dish from the oven and remove foil. Combine the melted butter and bread crumbs. Spread over the tomato mixture.

Return the dish to the oven, uncovered, and bake 15 additional minutes.

Coleslaw

Serves: 4
Prep time: 30 mins
Cook time: none

½ red or white cabbage,
  shredded finely
½ red onion, finely sliced
1 carrot, grated
3 tbsp mayonnaise
1 tbsp lemon juice
1 tsp white wine vinegar
1 tbsp wholegrain mustard
1 tsp sugar to taste
Salt and black pepper to taste

Put the chopped cabbage, carrot and onion into a big bowl.

In a smaller bowl, mix together the mayonnaise, lemon juice, vinegar and wholegrain mustard. Season with salt and freshly ground black pepper and stir to thoroughly combine. Pour over the vegetables.

Toss the slaw with the dressing. Serve immediately or cover and leave in the fridge for up to 2 days until ready to use.

Lord Astor's Salad Dressing

Prep time: 10 mins

4 dsp white or red wine vinegar
1 tsp olive oil
2 dsp caster sugar
2 tsps finely chopped onion
Pinch of salt

Mix the mustard, vinegar, sugar and salt together in a bowl. Gradually add the olive oil, mixing all the time. Then add in the chopped onion, check seasoning and add more salt and pepper if desired.

Oswald Birley's Salad Dressing

Prep time: 10 mins

2 tsps Dijon mustard
1 tsp Tarragon mustard
2 tsps white or red wine vinegar
4-6 tbsps good olive oil
1 tbsp chopped chervil
1 tbsp chopped chives
1 tbsp chopped celery tops
Salt, pepper and sugar to taste

Mix the mustard, pepper and salt together in a bowl. Add in the vinegar and mix. Gradually add the olive oil, mixing all the time, until a thick emulsion is achieved. Then add in the chopped herbs and sugar, with more salt and pepper to taste. Use with 'picked, dry lettuce leaves.'

Waldorf Salad

Serves: 2
Prep time: 30 mins
Cook time: none

1 red apple, sliced
1 stick celery, chopped
200g/ 1 ⅓ cups cooked
    shredded chicken
100g/ ½ cup chopped walnuts
A handful fresh rocket/arugula
    leaves

MAYONNAISE DRESSING
2 egg yolks
1 tsp Dijon mustard
290ml/1 ¼ cup vegetable oil
Juice of 1 lemon
Salt and pepper to taste

For the salad, put all the salad ingredients into a large bowl and mix well.

For the mayonnaise dressing, put the egg yolks and mustard into a mixing bowl and whisk together. Gradually add the vegetable oil, whisking continuously until all the oil is mixed in. Whisk the lemon juice into the mixture and season with salt and freshly ground black pepper.

To serve, mix the mayonnaise with the salad and spoon into a serving bowl.

Beetroot with Yoghurt and Dill

Serves: 4
Prep time: 30 mins
Cook time: none

6 good sized fresh beetroot,
    cooked, peeled and quartered
250g/ 1 cup whole milk plain yoghurt
125g/ ½ cup sour cream
3 cloves garlic, crushed
½ bunch fresh dill
½ bunch fresh chives
¼ red onion, finely chopped
3 tbsp lemon juice
Salt and black pepper to taste

Mix all the ingredients except the beetroot together, reserving some dill and chives for garnish. Adjust seasonings to taste. Arrange all the quartered beetroot on a flat serving dish, spoon over the yoghurt mixture carefully and scatter the green herbs over the top.

Summer Salad

Serves: 4
Prep: 20 mins
Chill Time: 30 mins

4 spring onions, finely sliced
1 bunch radishes, sliced thinly
4 celery sticks, finely sliced
2 red Romaine lettuce, root
    removed and leaves left whole
Small bunch of watercress tips.
    discard the thick stems
Small bunch chives, finely chopped
150g/ ¾ cup creme fraiche
Juice of ½ a lemon
1 tsp English mustard
½ tsp caraway seeds, crushed
    in a pestle and mortar
Sea salt and black pepper to taste

Layer the romaine leaves on a large flat plate then scatter over the spring onions, radishes, celery. In a bowl, mix the crème fraiche, English mustard, caraway seeds and lemon juice until well combined.

Drizzle the dressing over the salad mix then scatter with watercress tips and chopped chives. Season with sea salt and black pepper then serve.

Pullman Salad

Serves: 4
Prep: 10 mins

4 sticks celery, sliced thinly
1 cucumber, peeled, deseeded
    and cut into semi circles
1 bunch radishes, sliced thinly
½ red onion, sliced thinly
200g/ ¾ cup Roquefort cheese
4 Little Gem lettuce, cut into
    quarters lengthways
Olive oil

This salad is best served cold so prepare at the last minute with ingredients that have been refrigerated.

Lay the little gem quarters over the base of a large flat plate.

In a bowl, mix the celery, cucumber, radishes and red onion, and then scatter over the little gem leaves.

Drizzle with olive oil, then dot the crumbled Roquefort evenly over the salad. Serve immediately

CHAPTER 4

NANCY ASTOR

'Oh, Mrs Langhorne,' a friend said to my mother, 'your husband has such lovely eyes.' 'Don't be fooled by that,' came the soft reply, 'he looks just the same way at a batter cake.'

DESSERTS

'I hated [agreeing the day's menus each morning],' declared Nancy Tree on her arrival at Kelmarsh Hall, 'so I sat down for two weeks and made a menu book. I listed first courses, main courses and all the desserts. I did it for lunch, dinner, teas, high teas, suppers before the theatre, Christmas dinner. I would tell my cook, 'Any of these things suit me if you serve them just as I've written them down.' Isabella Tree.

There was no question that, while neither aunt nor niece could boil an egg, they certainly knew how food should be prepared and how to give the right instructions to their cooks. This they had both learned at Mirador, for while Nancy Astor had made her life in England, her niece had suffered a double tragedy when both her parents, Thomas Moncure and Lizzie Perkins, had died within weeks of each other in 1914. Lizzie was the eldest of the Langhorne children, and so another aunt, the famous beauty Irene Gibson, took Nancy with her to live and be launched in society in New York, spending the summers at Mirador. 'Mirador, Mirth and Misery, my aunts used to say. Mirador is deep in me I feel it in my bones even now. Nothing else has ever been as important. I'm not really interested in England or America, only in Virginia and Mirador. They're my roots and my soul.'

Like her aunt before her, Nancy absorbed Chillie's culinary interests. 'My grandmother Nanaire ran Mirador, but it was Grandfather who ordered the special Virginian delicacies (like pickled watermelon rinds and black bean soup) that he loved. He knew a lot about food and how it ought to be cooked.' On turnip tops he loved garlic sherry, which Nancy's sister, Alice Winn, remembered he offered to guests as well, saying, 'Have a little suspicion of garlic.' 'When he went to Richmond to stay with my mother' Nancy said, 'he invariably brought country butter and delicious sausage meat in a tin pail.' Her grandmother Nanaire's decorating was simple and elegant: 'In the winter the storm doors were put on the front and back. The rooms were heated by log fires and on the hall table stood a basket of apples (those tiny rose ones that only grow in old orchards).' After the sudden death of Nancy's first husband, Marshall Field's heir Henry Field, and her remarriage to his first cousin Ronald Tree, she bought Mirador from her aunt Phyllis Brand, who had inherited it. This was Nancy's first project, and she soon hired William Adams Delano to rebuild and hollow out the centre for a hanging staircase. She made certain that all the family could continue to return to the foot of the Blue Ridge Mountains, however far away life had taken them. Ronnie's political ambitions were to wrench Nancy away from Virginia too. In 1926, she and Ronnie arrived in England to spend a season hunting with the Pytchley in Leicestershire, and rented Kelmarsh Hall nearby.

Nancy's skill transformed Kelmarsh into an oasis of taste and comfort – much like her aunt had done at Cliveden – and thanks to the more relaxed spirit of the Twenties, she could also initiate major reforms in the kitchen. Armed with her copy of the Mirador Cookbook and her New York cook Elise du Four, the menus at Kelmarsh underwent a dramatic change. Interspersed with traditional French dishes, dinner could comprise of Fish Chowder, followed by *Poulets Rôtis au Cresson*, Vegetables, Salad and Orange Mist for dessert. Or consommé with poached egg, followed by Roast Loin of Pork with creamed celery and Pommes d'Anna ending in 'Linger Tart' (Johnson, the Mirador cook's interpretation of Linzertorte).

In this chapter for Desserts, recipes collected by friends began to appear, (possibly because England was and is famous for its puddings) and some from travels in Italy and Bavaria. Mrs Randolph Meade's Blackberry cake, Lady Adare's Mousseline de Caramel, Lord Berners's Pouding Louise p102 and Lady Cranborne's chocolate mousse p107 are recorded, as is a beautiful Mokka Crème p108, (which came from the Kurhaus Hoven spa in Freiburg where the Astors would go for a rest cure every now and then), Sacher Cake from Vienna p106 and Zabaglione from Italy p99.

BELOW: Nancy Lancaster at Kelmarsh Hall in 1950, having married her third husband Colonel 'Jubie' Lancaster, from whom she and Ronald Tree had originally leased Kelmarsh from 1928 until 1933.

Blueberry Pie

1.5kg/3lb 4oz fresh or frozen
  blueberries
12 tablespoons/ 150g caster/
  superfine sugar
2 tablespoons corn starch/
  cornflour
225g/ 1 ¾ cups flour
140g/ ⅝ cup cold unsalted butter
Pinch of salt
6 teaspoons cold water
3-6 tablespoons milk
1 tablespoon double/heavy cream
1 large egg yolk
Caster/superfine sugar to serve

Sieve the flour and salt into a bowl and fold in the butter until the mixture is course and fine, like breadcrumbs. Then add the cold water to the flour mixture and knead it in until the dough is firm and the colour even. Wrap in plastic wrap and place in the fridge for at least ½ an hour.

Place the berries into a saucepan over a medium heat and, using a potato masher, mash the berries to release the juices, and add cornflour. Continue to cook, stirring frequently and occasionally mashing until around half of the berries are broken down and the mixture is generally thickened and reduced (takes about 8 mins). Let it all cool.

Preheat the oven to 220°C.

Divide the pastry in two and take one half and roll it out into a 12-inch circle. Add a few sprinkles of flour to keep the dough from sticking. Gently fold in half and place onto an 8-9 inch plate, lining up the fold with the centre of the pan. Gently unfold the pastry and press down to line the dish with the dough. Add the fruit filling to the dough-lined pie pan. Trim any excess dough with a knife, leaving a ¾ inch overhang.

Roll out a second disk of dough, as before. Gently turn over onto the top of the berries in the pie. Pinch the top and bottom of the dough together. Trim excess dough with a knife, leaving a ¾ inch overhang. Fold the dough under itself so that the edge of the fold is flush with the edge of the pan. Flute the edges using your thumb and forefinger.

Beat the egg yolk with the milk and cream, brush onto the surface of the pie with a pastry brush. Prick the surface of the pastry lightly before placing the pie in the oven to let any excess steam out. Cook for 20-30 mins. Slide on to a serving plate, dust with caster sugar and serve.

Lady Astor's Apricot Brown Betty

Serves 4-6
Prep time: 30 mins
Cook time: 40 mins

325g/3 cups day old bread
3 tbsps butter
225g/ 1 ½ cups dried apricots –
   soaked
95g/ ¾ cup caster/superfine sugar
½ tsp ground cinnamon

Preheat oven to 180 C/ 360 F. Butter a rectangular or oval ovenproof dish.

Cut the bread into dice and sauté in butter until brown. Drain the soaked apricots and slice thin, then dredge with the sugar mixed with cinnamon. Cover the bottom of the baking dish with bread. Add the fruit and remaining bread in alternate layers, saving a little bread to put on top. Bake for 30 minutes, or until golden on top.

Apple Charlotte with Apricot sauce

Serves: 4
Prep time: 30 mins
Cook time: 40 mins

900g/2lb cooking apples,
   peeled, cored and cut small
120g/ ⅝ cups caster/superfine sugar
120g/ ½ cup butter
4 tbsp water
Juice of ½ lemon
Approx 8 thin slices dry white
   bread, crusts removed

APRICOT SAUCE
250g/ ½ lb dried apricots
70g/ ⅓ cup caster/superfine sugar
6 tbsp water
1 tbsp lemon juice

Preheat oven to 180 C/ 356 F. Butter a mould or soufflé dish about 7.5cm deep.

Put the sliced apples in a heavy pan with the sugar, about a third of the butter and 4 tbsps water. Cook on a low heat, covered, until soft. Uncover the pan and carry on cooking until a thick purée forms. Add the lemon juice.

Cut the bread to fit the mould, then melt the rest of the butter and dip the slices to coat on both sides, then back into the mould to fit. Fill the lined dish with the apple purée and cover with a lid of more butter coated bread. Bake in the oven for 35-40 minutes until golden brown on top. Leave to cool slightly, then turn out onto a flat dish to serve.

APRICOT SAUCE
Soak the apricots in water for an hour, then cook slowly until tender. Blend in a mixer then add the sugar and water to the pulp in a pan, and cook slowly for 5 minutes. Add the lemon juice, then serve.

Crêpes Normandes (Thin Apple Pancakes)

Makes 4-6 pancakes
Prep time: 20 mins
(plus an hour for batter to stand)
Cook time: 20-30 minutes

4 tbsp plain flour
2 eggs
180ml/ ¾ cup whole milk
Pinch of salt
3 dessert apples, peeled,
  cored and sliced thin
120g/ ⅓ cup caster/superfine sugar
75g butter

Make the batter first, so that it can stand for an hour before using. Stir the flour and salt together in a large bowl, make a well and crack both eggs into it. Stir again to a stiff mixture, then gradually add the milk, stirring all the time so the batter becomes smooth with no lumps. Let it stand for an hour.

Melt the butter in one frying pan and put a quarter of the apple slices in it, and cook for about 2-3 minutes. Then add enough batter on top of them to make a thin pancake. Fry slowly until brown, then flip and sprinkle sugar evenly on this side. When pancake is cooked, turn and sprinkle sugar on the other side and slide onto a serving dish. Repeat until the rest of the ingredients are used up.

Pommes Bonne Femme (Baked Apples)

Serves: 4
Prep time: 30 mins
Cook time: 20-30 mins

4 large baking apples
4 thick slices white bread
120g/ ½ cup butter at room
  temperature
170g/ ¾ cup soft brown sugar

Preheat the oven to 180 C/ 356 F.

Cut four large rounds out of the white bread. Core the apples, then mix the butter and sugar to a paste and fill the apple centres with the mixture. Pile it also on top of the apples and stand them on the bread circles (croûtes) in a baking tin. Bake in the oven, basting a couple of times, for about 20-30 minutes until soft and the croûtes are golden brown.

Then put the croûtes on top of the apples when serving, and fill the middle of the dish with hot whipped cream in which the rest of the baking caramel is mixed, after pouring some over the apples.

Individual Marmalade Soufflés

Serves: 4
Prep : 20 mins
Cook : 30 mins

4 medium oranges
150ml/ ⅔ cup whole milk
2 medium eggs, separated
6 level tbsp caster/superfine sugar
2 level tbsp plain flour
2 level tbsp fine-cut marmalade

Preheat the oven to 180°C/350°F/Gas Mark 4.

Slice the tops off 4 of the oranges and then scoop out all the flesh and juice into a sieve over a bowl. Squeeze out the juice from the pulp and reserve. Place the scooped-out oranges on to a baking tray, cutting a sliver off the bottoms if wobbly.

Measure milk in a measuring jug and make it up to 200ml (7fl oz) with the orange juice.

In a small pan, whisk the egg yolks with 4 tbsp of the sugar until smooth, then whisk in the flour.

Put the pan on a low heat and then gradually add the milk-and-orange mixture, whisking all the time. Heat for 1-2 mins, until the mixture thickens, then leave to cool. Add the marmalade to the custard and whisk again.

Whisk the egg whites in a bowl until they become foamy, then add the 2 remaining tbsp of sugar and whisk again, until it forms stiff peaks. Fold the custard mixture into the egg white, being careful to keep in the incorporated air and taking care not to over-mix.

Divide mixture between the scooped-out oranges. Fill up to top and flatten with a spatula.

Bake in the centre of the oven for about 25 mins. They should be golden on top and just firm to the touch when lightly pressed. Remove from the oven and serve immediately.

Orange Mist

Serves: 4 - 6
Prep time: 20 mins,
plus 30 mins cooling time
Chill time: overnight

¾ tbsp powdered gelatine
500ml/ 2 cups double/heavy
  or whipping cream
250ml/ 1 cup fresh orange juice
1 tbsp lemon juice
35g/ ⅓ cup icing (powdered)
  sugar

Sprinkle the gelatine over ¼ of the cup of orange juice, then tip into a saucepan with the remaining juice, including the lemon juice. Heat until the gelatine is dissolved then let stand to cool. Whip the cream,during which slowly add the icing sugar making a crème Chantilly. Then strain the juice and gelatine mixture through a sieve into the cream. Carefully fold together and then put into a ring mould or any container that will do for serving. Chill overnight and present garnished with fresh fruit.

Ditchley Crème Brûlée

Serves: 4
Prep time: 40 mins
Chill time: 4 hours

500ml/ 2 cups double/heavy cream
5 whole eggs
5 egg yolks
20g caster/superfine sugar
Half a vanilla pod (optional)
4 tbsp Demerara or light brown sugar

In a bowl over a saucepan of simmering water (or bain-marie) warm the cream. Add the eggs, egg yolks, sugar and scrape the vanilla seeds out of the pod into the mixture and add the pod itself. Continue cooking gently until the mixture has thickened enough to coat the back of the wooden spoon. Strain the cream through a fine sieve into a large soufflé dish or mould and leave to chill for at least 4 hours. Then sprinkle the demerara sugar on top of the chilled cream, set the dish or mould on top of a bed of ice cubes on a grill pan and place under a hot grill until the sugar has caramelized. (A kitchen blowtorch will also do the job). Put back in the refridgerator to cool again until needed.

Raspberry Parfait with Strawberry Sauce

Serves: 6
Prep time: 40 mins
Cook time: 6 hours
chilling and freezing

115g/ ⅝ cup caster/superfine sugar
4 egg yolks
200g/ 1 ½ cups fresh raspberries
142ml/ ½ cup double/heavy cream
1 tbsp kirsch

STRAWBERRY & RASPBERRY SAUCE
225g/ 1 ¾ cups fresh raspberries
300g/ 2 ¼ cups fresh strawberries
2 tbsp icing (powdered) sugar
1 tbsp kirsch

Put the sugar in a pan with 115ml water and dissolve over a low heat. Meanwhile, put the egg yolks in a bowl over a pan of simmering water. Using an electric whisk, whip the yolks until pale and creamy. Add the warm sugar syrup slowly to the egg yolks, whisking all the time.

Remove bowl from the pan and continue to whisk at a high speed for a minute, then reduce to a medium speed for 3-4 minutes. Reduce again and whisk at low speed for 5 minutes. The mixture will double in bulk. Chill for 30 minutes. Oil and line a 900g loaf tin with grease-proof paper. Purée the raspberries in a blender. Push through a sieve. Whisk the cream and kirsch until it forms soft peaks, then fold into the egg mousse, followed by the raspberry purée. Pour into the tin. Cover with a sheet of oiled grease-proof paper. Freeze for 4-5 hours.

To make the sauce, purée the berries in a blender. Push through a sieve. Add the kirsch and sugar. Chill. Loosen the parfait with a knife. Invert on to a plate. Peel off the paper and slice. Serve with the sauce and, if you like, more fresh fruit.

Zabaglione

Serves: 4
Prep time: 10 mins
Cook time: 20 mins

4 eggs
6 tsps caster/superfine sugar
4 tbsp sherry or Madeira
4 tbsp hot whole milk

Heat the milk. In a bowl beat the eggs with the sugar until pale and foamy, then add the sherry/Madeira and the hot milk. Place the bowl over a saucepan of boiling water and whisk it until it thickens and becomes foamy, but do not let it boil. Serve immediately.

'This is particularly good served with the green figs that are now to be had in tins or bottles'.

Pumpkin Pie

Serves: 6- 8
Prep time: 40 mins and 1 hour chilling
Cook time: 50 mins

750g/ 1lb 10oz pumpkin, peeled, deseeded and cut into chunks
350g / 10oz sweet shortcrust pastry (see Damson Tart for recipe)
140g/ ¾ cup caster/superfine sugar
175ml/ 1 ⅓ cups whole milk
25g/ 2 tbsp butter, melted
2 eggs, beaten
½ tsp salt
½ tsp fresh nutmeg, grated
1 tsp cinnamon
1 tbsp icing (powdered) sugar

Preheat oven to 180 C/350 F. Grease a loose-bottomed flan tin 20cm wide, 4cm deep. Place the pumpkin in a large pan, cover with water and bring to the boil. Cover with a lid and simmer for 15 minutes until tender. Drain and allow to cool. Roll out the pastry and line the flan tin. Put in the freezer for 15 minutes, then line with baking parchment or tin foil and baking beans. Bake in the oven for 15 minutes. Remove the paper and beans, and cook for a further 10 minutes until pale golden. Remove from the oven and allow to cool.

Increase the oven to 220 C/ 425 F. With a hand blender or food processor purée the pumpkin. In a separate bowl, combine the sugar, salt, nutmeg and half the cinnamon. Mix in the beaten eggs, melted butter and milk then add to the pumpkin puree and stir to combine. Pour into the tart shell and bake for 10 minutes, then reduce the oven heat down to 180 C/350 F and bake for a further 35-40 minutes until the filling has just set.

Leave to cool, then mix the remaining cinnamon with the icing sugar and dust over the pie.

Lord Berners's Pouding Louise

Serves: 6- 8
Prep time: 30 mins and 30 mins chilling time
Cook time: 1 hour

PASTRY BASE:
110g/ ¾ cup plain flour
75g/ ⅓ cup butter, chilled
35g/ 3 tbsp caster/superfine sugar
35g/ 3 tbsp ground almonds
1 tsp vanilla essence
2 tsps double/heavy cream

FILLING:
75g/ ⅓ cup butter at room temperature
75g/ 6 tbsp caster/superfine sugar
30g/ 2 tbsp plain flour
1 small jar redcurrant jelly

Preheat oven to 180 C/350 F. Grease a loose-bottomed flan tin 20cm wide, 4cm deep.

For the pastry, in a large bowl rub together the flour, butter, sugar and almonds. Bring together to form a dough with the vanilla essence and cream. Add more cream if the dough is still too dry. Wrap in clingfilm and refridgerate for at least half an hour.

Roll out the pastry and line the flan tin. Put in the freezer while making the filling. Cream together the butter and sugar until pale and fluffy, then fold in the flour. Take out the flan tin from the freezer and line the bottom with the redcurrant jelly. Spread the mixture over this and bake in the oven for 1 hour or until the top has formed a hard, golden crust. Serve warm.

Linzertorte (or 'Linger Tarte')

Serves: 6- 8
Prep time: 30 mins and
30 mins chilling time
Cook time: 1 hour

220g/1 ½ cups plain flour
220g/1 cup butter
220g/1 cup caster/superfine sugar
220g/1 cup ground almonds
75g/ ½ cup finely chopped
   lemon peel
1 egg
2 tbsp kirsch (optional)
½ tsp ground cinnamon
450g/1 1/3 cups raspberry jam
Egg and milk mixed for glazing

Linger Tarte was how Johnson, the Mirador cook, pronounced Linzertorte.

Preheat oven to 180 C/350 F.

Grease a loose-bottomed flan tin 20cm wide, 4cm deep. Rub together the flour, butter, sugar and almonds with the tips of the fingers in a large bowl. Add the lemon peel, egg and kirsch (if using) and combine to form a dough. If not using kirsch, add a little milk to combine. Wrap in plastic and chill for half an hour.

Roll out the dough and line the tin, cover with the jam and with the remaining pastry cut strips to form a lattice criss-crossing the surface of the jam. Brush the pastry lattice with the egg and milk mixture. Place in the oven and bake for about an hour or until crisp and golden brown.

Damson Tart

Serves: 4
Prep time: 20 mins and 1 hour chilling time
Cook time: 1 hour

PASTRY BASE:
120g/1 cup plain flour
115g/ ½ cup butter, chilled
1 ½ tbsp caster/superfine sugar
Pinch salt
2-3 tbsp ice water

FILLING:
220g/1 cup caster/superfine sugar
220g/1 cup butter,
   room temperature
5 eggs, separated
220g/1 cup damson jam
1 tsp vanilla essence

Preheat oven to 180 C/350 F. Grease a loose-bottomed flan tin 20cm wide, 4cm deep.

For the pastry: in a large bowl rub together the flour, butter, sugar and salt either by hand or process in a food processor. Add enough of the water to bring together to form dough. Wrap in clingfilm and refrigerate for at least 1 hour.

Roll out the pastry and line the flan tin. Put in the freezer while making the filling.

FILLING
Cream the butter and sugar together with an electric mixer or whisk, until pale and fluffy. Beat in the egg yolks. Beat the egg whites until peaks form and fold these carefully into the mixture. Then fold in the damson jam. Beat all together until very light. Add the vanilla essence and turn into the pastry shell. Bake in the oven for about an hour or until golden brown.

'You Cannot Leave Me Alone'

Serves: 4
Prep time: 25 min
Cook time: 1 hour

113g/1 stick unsalted butter
225g/1 cup caster/superfine sugar
125g/1 cup plain/all purpose flour
2 teaspoons baking powder
185ml/¾ cup whole milk
2 large eggs
400g of either tinned or fresh,
  pitted cherries with juice

This dish resembles a traditional French cherry Clafoutis, but was so named by the family because no one could stop eating it. Apples, pears or apricots could also be used if cherries are unavailable.

Preheat the oven to 160 c/325 f and butter a glass or china flat, oval baking dish.

If using fresh cherries, stone them and put in a small saucepan with a sprinkling of sugar and heat slowly. Cook on a low heat until the cherries are soft and the juice begins to run.

In a bowl, mix the flour, sugar, baking powder together. Make a well and drop the eggs into it. Stir to combine, don't worry if it looks lumpy.

Gradually beat in the milk until the batter is smooth.

Transfer to the flat glass or china baking dish.

Melt the butter and pour this over the flour & sugar mixture, but do not stir it. On top of this pour the canned or fresh cherries.

Bake in the oven for an hour, until the sponge feels firm to the touch and there is shrinkage at the sides.

Serve warm with thick cream.

Chocolate Cake
a la Sacher

Serves: 4
Prep time: 40 mins
Cook time: 20-30 mins, then leave
until the following day

100g/ ¾ cup dark chocolate
  (or chocolate chips)
100g/ ½ cup caster/superfine sugar
100g/ ½ cup butter
100g/ ¾ cup plain flour
50g/ ½ cup ground almonds
6 eggs, separated
6 tbsp apricot jam

Preheat the oven to 180 c /350 F. Grease a 20cm/8in round cake tin and line the base with parchment paper.

Melt the chocolate over a pan of simmering water then remove from the heat to cool. Whisk the egg whites until stiff. Cream the butter and mix it with the chocolate, the sugar and the egg yolks. Fold in the flour and the almonds, then fold in the whisked egg whites. Pour the batter into the tin and bake in the oven for 20-30 minutes, until the top is firm and the sides are coming away from the tin. Leave to cool, then turn out of the tin onto a wire rack. When completely cold wrap in clingfilm until the next day.

The next day, divide the cake into two layers. Spread with the jam and place the two layers back together. Coat the cake with chocolate icing (see below).

Chocolate Icing

Serves: 4
Prep time: 40 mins
Chill time: 4 hours

75g/ ½ cup dark chocolate
  (or chocolate chips)
75g/ ½ cup icing (powdered) sugar
6 tbsp boiling water
2 tbsp icing (powdered) sugar

Melt the chocolate over in a bowl over a saucepan of simmering water (bain marie). Stir in the icing sugar. In a smaller saucepan boil the 6 tbsp of water with the 2 tbsp of icing sugar. Pour this syrup into the chocolate mixture, stirring briskly until the icing is sufficiently thick. While it is still hot, pour the icing over the cake, and leave to set.

Ditchley Pots au Crème de Chocolat

Serves: 4
Prep time: 20 mins
Cook time: 30 mins
Chill time: at least 4 hours

120ml/ ½ cup whole milk
2 eggs
1 ½ tablespoons cornflour/cornstarch
3 tbsp granulated/white sugar
½ tsp salt
1 tsp vanilla essence
1 egg white, whisked
60g/ ¼ cup dark chocolate

Melt the chocolate in a bowl over a simmering saucepan of water, and set aside to cool a little. Beat the eggs with the sugar and salt with an electric whisk until pale and foamy. Dissolve the cornstarch in a little water. Heat the milk in a saucepan but do not boil, and add this slowly to the eggs and sugar mixture whisking as it combines.

Whisk in the cornstarch, and then add the mixture to the chocolate. Return the chocolate mixture to the bain marie and cook for about 10-15 minutes longer until thick and smooth. Finally, add in the whisked egg white and vanilla essence. Pour into 4 individual cups or ramekins, and chill until set.

Lady Cranborne's Chocolate Mousse

Serves: 6- 8
Prep time: 30 mins
Chill time: at least 4 hours

500ml/ 2 cups double/heavy cream
220g/ 1 ¾ cup grated dark chocolate
2 egg whites
1 tbsp icing (powdered) sugar

Whip the egg whites until stiff and peaks form. In a separate bowl whip the cream to the same consistency. Fold the egg whites into the cream, then fold in half the grated chocolate and icing sugar to taste. Put into one glass serving dish or individual glasses. Sprinkle the remaining chocolate over the surface and refrigerate for at least 3-4 hours.

Mokka Crème

Serves 6-8
Prep time: 30 mins
Chill time: 4 hours

½ pint/ 2 ¼ cups very strong coffee
150g caster/superfine sugar
8 egg yolks
1 pint/ 4 ½ cups whole milk
12 leaves gelatine
1 pint/ 4 ½ cups heavy/double cream
1 tablespoon cornflour

This recipe was served at the Kurhaus Hoven Spa in Freiburg, Germany, where the Astors often went for a rest cure. It must have been a favourite, as the recipe was obtained from the spa's Austrian chef and added to the Mirador Cook Book.

Equipment: 1 x 2pint shaped jelly mould, or 2 1 pint shaped jelly moulds. Separate the eggs and in a bowl, beat the yolks with the sugar until pale and thick.

Boil the milk and add to the yolk and sugar mixture, beating well. Return the mixture from the bowl to the saucepan and bring up to the boil again. Remove from the heat, and add the strong coffee together with the gelatin leaves, and mix well.

Leave the saucepan to cool, or even in the fridge, and when completely cold, whip the cream lightly and fold this carefully into the mixture, making sure it is completely absorbed.

Pour the mixture into the jelly mould and put back in the fridge for at least 4 hours.

When set, run a knife gently around the inside perimeter, put a plate on top and turn the mould upside down onto the plate. Tap to release. Decorate with whipped cream and some whole coffee beans.

CHAPTER 5

NANCY ASTOR

"Winston, if I were your wife
I'd put poison in your tea."

WINSTON CHURCHILL

"Nancy, if I were your husband
I'd drink it."

BREAD, BISCUITS & CAKES

Nancy Lancaster had a wonderful lady's maid called Winnie, who was with her for years and years (she retired at 90). One day she fainted in the kitchen and when she came round asked 'Where am I?' in a panic. Aunt Nancy said 'In Hell, as I'm looking after you'. Jane Churchill.

Tea at four o'clock in the afternoon has always played a major part in English country house life, but has never been much of a fixture in America. At Mirador, cake was eaten after dinner, as a dessert, and the children had their 'high tea' (a mixture of tea and supper, in the same way that brunch is a mixture of breakfast and lunch) at around 6pm. As Nancy Lancaster recalled 'at Mirador there was a table where we grandchildren had our supper of milk, bread and butter, damson preserve and a scrambled egg which we had found fresh, preferably of a guinea fowl, duck or turkey. On the porch Emily Pate, our housekeeper, sat with her sewing machine, keeping an eye on us.' The grown-ups would have the same supper every night; corn bread and eggs, raw tomatoes, wheaten biscuits and molasses. They rarely ate meat in the evenings. It was at Kelmarsh Hall where Nancy Tree was initiated into the ritual 'tyranny of meals' that formed the basis of English country house life, and tea –

particularly for the hunting community – was a vital part of it. Nancy's hunting teas were laid out in the pink hall at the end of a day in front of a roaring fire, and the artist Sir Alfred Munnings recalled in his memoirs 'the large tea table – eggs, fried sausages, toast. A party of men and women back from the chase – Earl Beatty in his shirtsleeves and yellow waistcoat, his coat slung over a chair, attacking sausages'. An array of Virginian drop scones and cinnamon teacakes as well as chocolate cake and shortbread were served, together with both Indian and China leaf tea.

As blissful as life at Kelmarsh was, and despite Ronnie's appointment as Member of Parliament for nearby Market Harborough, he had nonetheless fallen in love with another house, Ditchley Park, near Charlbury in Oxfordshire. To Nancy's shock he announced in 1933 that he had bought it, having only viewed it once with her. Together they set about performing the same miracle at Ditchley as they had at Kelmarsh, only on a far grander scale. Reams have been written about this house, a collaboration of style with Sybil Colefax and Stephane Boudin of Jansen in Paris, which earned Nancy the reputation of having the 'finest taste of almost anyone in the world.' Debo, the Duchess of Devonshire was to recall, ' I realise now that Ditchley taught me an invaluable lesson – to notice, to look and try to absorb and remember what was beautiful.' The years 1935-1939 saw a glittering array of weekend guest, parties and Ascot weeks at Ditchley, culminating in a spectacular ball in June 1937 for a thousand guests. According to Cecil Beaton Ditchley was 'an enormous eighteenth century doll's house of honey-coloured stone...through the tall windows the gold ceiling and chandeliers sparkled. Canopied beds could be glimpsed upstairs; the great front doors stood open to the steady stream of guests and the balmy velvet evening.' It was Nancy's consummate skills as a hostess that propelled Ditchley into the front line of the war effort as dark clouds gathered over Europe. Ronnie was among a small group of politicians who saw the rising Nazi party as a threat to Britain and he became a member of anti-appeasement MPs who included Anthony Eden and Duff Cooper. As a result, Winston Churchill and his wife Clementine began dining at Ditchley (and the Trees' house in London) from 1937 onwards, and it seemed only natural for Ronnie to offer Ditchley as a weekend retreat for the Prime Minister when Chequers (the country house which all British Prime Ministers are allowed to use) was found to be too exposed to Luftwaffe bombardment.

Throughout all, the Mirador cookbook 'continued to dominate the elaborate meals that Nancy had typed and punched into a large ring-binder for her chef.' writes Isabella Tree, 'Luncheon Menu 6 began 'Oeufs en Cocotte, followed by 'Creamed Sweetbreads and Spoonbread made with Grits' with 'Apple Tapioca' for dessert'. For having purchased Mirador from her aunt Phyllis Brand in 1922, Nancy and Ronald had initiated substantial redecorating works prior to arriving in Britain, and everything she had achieved at Kelmarsh and Ditchley was that dream of Mirador under English skies: a luxurious simplicity, a cosiness amongst the grandeur revealing a lightness of touch that was her genius.

OPPOSITE: Picnic lunch at Ditchley Park, 1934. From left to right, Elizabeth Cavendish, Duff Cooper, Hermione Lee, Lady Diana Cooper.

Popovers

Makes: 12
Prep time: 10 mins plus
1 hour to rest the batter
Cook time: 25 mins

3 eggs beaten lightly in a
  mixing bowl
185g/ 1 ½ cups plain
  (all purpose) flour
½ tsp baking powder
¼ tsp salt
1 tbsp melted unsalted butter
250ml/ 1 cup whole milk
A 12-hole deep ringed muffin tray

(The British know these as Yorkshire puddings but popovers can also be eaten with jam or cheese.)

Preheat the oven to 200 C/ 395 F.

Sift the flour, baking powder and the salt into a large bowl.

Warm the milk and add to the beaten eggs, then add to the flour in the large bowl and beat well with an electric whisk or hand whisk, until smooth and any lumps have evened out.

Rest the batter for an hour.

Brush muffin moulds with melted butter, divide the batter equally between the moulds and bake for 20 – 25 minutes until well risen and golden.

Serve immediately while hot.

Whole Wheat Biscuits

Makes 12
Prep time: 20 mins
Cook time: 12-14 mins

225g/1 ¾ cups wholemeal/whole wheat flour
225g/1 ¾ cups plain flour
115g/½ cup unsalted very cold butter, cut into pieces
225ml/¾ cup buttermilk or milk with 1 tbsp lemon juice added
1 tbsp baking powder
½ tsp bicarbonate of soda
2 tsp caster/superfine sugar
½ tsp salt

Preheat oven to 220 C/425 F.

In a large bowl whisk flours, baking powder, bicarbonate of soda, sugar, and salt. Cut in butter until mixture resembles coarse meal. Add buttermilk to dry ingredients, stirring until dry ingredients are moistened.

Turn the dough out onto a lightly floured surface and knead lightly 4 to 5 times. Roll or pat dough out to about 2.5-cm thickness. Cut with a biscuit cutter and place on an ungreased baking tray. Bake for about 12 to 14 minutes or until brown. Serve warm.

Beaten Biscuits (from Foxcroft, Middleburg, VA)

Makes 50
Prep time: 40 mins
Cook time: 15-20 mins

580g/ 4 ½ cups plain flour
30g/ 2 tbsp butter
150ml/ ¾ cup ice cold milk
1 tsp salt

These resemble hard biscuits eaten with cheese or thin slices of ham. Foxcroft is the school where America's elite families sent their daughters, including Nancy Lancaster, and she brought this recipe home with her.

Preheat oven to 230 C/450 F. Grease 2 or 3 baking trays.

Sift the flour with the teaspoon of salt into a large bowl. Work in the butter with your fingers, and moisten with the teacup of cold milk until the dough forms. Turn out onto a floured, flat surface and knead until it becomes smooth and easy to handle.

With a mallet or wooden rolling pin, beat the dough a few times to form it into a rough rectangle. Fold the dough over and beat it out again. Repeat this process a few times until the dough becomes white and blisters form on the surface – about 15 minutes.

Roll out the dough until about 1cm thick and cut into 5cm rounds. Prick the top with a fork and place on the baking sheets. Bake in the oven for 15-20 minutes until light brown.

Bran Muffins

Makes 6
Prep time: 30 mins
Cook time: 20 mins

120g/ 1 cup Kellog's All Bran
120g/ 1 cup plain flour
125ml/ 1 cup buttermilk
   (or whole milk with a tablespoon
   of lemon juice)
40g/ 2 tablespoons butter or lard
30g/ ¼ cup caster/superfine sugar
1 egg
1 tsp baking powder
½ tsp bicarbonate of soda
¼ tsp salt
(Raisins or dates can be added
   if desired, about 100g/1 cup)

Preheat oven to 200 C/400 F. Oil a 6-cup muffin tray or use paper liners.

Cream the butter/lard and sugar with an electric whisk, then add the egg. Place a sieve over a separate bowl and sift the flour, soda, salt and baking powder into it. To the creamed mixture add the All-Bran, then the milk alternately with the dry flour ingredients.

Divide batter equally into the muffin tins, and bake for 20 minutes.

Waffles

Serves 4
Prep time: 30 mins
Cook time: 10-30 mins

3 eggs 'well beating or beaten'
360g/ 3 cups plain flour
1 pint/ 570 ml whole milk
110g/ 1 cup butter (melted)
1 tsp caster/superfine sugar
½ tsp salt

You will need a waffle maker, and preheat this to a medium setting. Preheat oven to low 140 C/275 F.

Mix the flour, baking powder, salt and granulated sugar in a large mixing bowl. Whisk in the eggs, milk and butter until well combined.

Ladle some of the batter into each well of the waffle maker, close the lid and cook for five minutes, or until golden-brown and crisp. Repeat the process until the batter is used up. Keep the waffles warm on the baking tray in the oven. Serve with whipped cream, berries and maple syrup – or just plain butter.

Spoon Bread

Serves 6-8
Prep time: 20 mins
Cook time: 35 mins

120g/ ¾ cup cornmeal
  (or polenta)
250ml/ 1 cup boiling water
3 tbsp melted butter
250ml/ 1 cup milk
2 large eggs
2 tsps baking powder
1 tsp salt

Similar to cornbread, spoon bread is more like a soufflé, and is scooped out of the dish with a spoon. Serve it as a side dish with any casserole or roast meat.

Preheat oven to 170 C/350 F. Grease an 8 x 8 inch square pan or oven dish.

Mix together in cornmeal and salt in a bowl, and gradually add the boiling water while whisking out any lumps. Add the melted butter and stir to blend. Let the mixture cool for 5 minutes.

Whisk in the milk. Then beat the eggs in a separate bowl and whisk these into the cornmeal mixture with an electric hand whisk. Pour the batter into the prepared dish and cook for about 35 minutes until set and lightly browned.

Batter Bread

Makes 1 one pan loaf
Prep time: 20 mins
Cook time: 30 mins

160g /1 cup cornmeal (or polenta)
500ml/ 2 cups boiling water
250ml/ 1 cup cold milk
2 eggs (unbeaten)
125ml/ ½ cup melted butter
1 tsp baking powder
½ tsp salt

Batter bread, a sort of cross between corn bread and custard, was another staple at Mirador. A visiting Englishman once amused both Nancys (and all of their relations) when he told his wife, "oh you must try this BATTLE bread. It's not half as nasty as it looks."

Preheat oven to 200 C/390 F. Oil a square baking pan.

Put the cornmeal in a large mixing bowl, and pour the boiling water over it. Stir to combine. Add the rest of the ingredients and mix them all together well.

Pour the batter into the greased pan, and bake in the oven for 30 minutes. When ready, leave to cool in the tin. When quite cold, invert onto a flat board and cut into squares.

English Scones

Makes: 6 large, 10 small
Prep time: 15 mins
Cook time: 10 mins

225g/ 1 ¾ cups plain flour
Pinch salt
½ tsp bicarbonate of soda
1 tsp baking powder
30g/ ¼ cup chilled butter
4 tbsp milk and water mixed
Milk for glazing

Preheat oven to 220 C/ 450 F. Flour a flat baking tray.

Sift the flour, salt, bicarbonate of soda and baking powder into a large bowl. Cut the butter into small squares and rub into the flour using hands. Gradually add milk and water, and mix together with a knife to form a soft ball of dough.

Knead on a floured surface briefly then roll out to ½ inch thick. Using a 2 inch pastry cutter cut out as many scones as possible. Roll up the trimmings and repeat. Place on the floured tray and brush the tops with milk. Bake in the oven for about 10 minutes until well risen and golden brown.

Clovelly Brown Scone Loaf

Serves: 4-6
Prep time: 30 mins
Cook time: 30 mins

450g/ 3 ½ cups wholemeal/ whole wheat flour
60g/ ¼ cup butter
60g/ ¼ cup caster/superfine sugar
60g/ ¼ cup sultanas/golden raisins
a pinch of salt
1 level teaspoon Bicarbonate of Soda
1 heaped teaspoon Cream of Tartar
300ml/ 10 fl oz milk
1 egg

Preheat oven to 180 c/360°f. Brush a baking tray lightly with oil.

In a large bowl, rub the butter into the flour, and add the sultanas, sugar, salt, Bicarbonate of Soda and Cream of Tartar.

Make a well in the centre of the dry mixture and pour in the milk. Bring the dough together in the bowl with a knife or your hands, and turn out onto a floured surface.

Roll out to half an inch thickness with a rolling pin and place on the baking sheet.

With a pizza cutter or knife, criss cross the dough lightly on the surface into four.

Paint with eggwash over the surface and bake in the oven for 30 minutes. When cooled a little, break into four pieces and serve hot.

Mrs Gibson's Thin & Crispy Corn Bread

Serves: 8
Prep: 10 mins
Cook time: 10 mins

2 tablespoons cornmeal
  or polenta
125ml/ ½ cup milk
⅛ teaspoon salt
½ teaspoon of caster/superfine sugar

Mrs Gibson's recipes feature quite regularly within the family cookbook, as she was known to have inherited Chillie's legendary interest in food and drink and kept a superb table of her own in New York.

You will need a cast iron frying pan/skillet that can be put in the oven. This must be well greased with butter or vegetable fat like Trex or Crisco.

Preheat oven to 200 c/425°f.

Mix the cornmeal/polenta, salt and sugar, then add the milk. Mix till smooth, then pour into the frying pan or skillet, making sure the pan is large enough so that the batter is thinly spread.

Cook in the hot oven for 8-10 minutes until nicely browned. Remove and slice into 8 servings.

Cornsticks

Makes: 18
Prep: 10 mins
Cook time: 10 mins

60ml/ ¼ cup plus 2 tablespoons
  vegetable oil, divided
200g/ 1½ cups plain yellow
  cornmeal or polenta
30g/ ¼ cup plain/all-purpose flour
3 tablespoons caster/superfine sugar
1 teaspoon bicarbonate of soda
½ teaspoon baking powder
½ teaspoon salt
1 cup whole buttermilk or milk
1 large egg

Not to be confused with corn dogs, these are in fact deliciously light 'fingers' of cornbread, baked in a specific pan with the bread moulds shaped like ears of corn. In Europe cornmeal is known as polenta.

Preheat oven to 200 c/425°f. Brush ¼ cup oil into wells of cast-iron corn stick pans, and place pans in oven to preheat.

In a large bowl, whisk together cornmeal or polenta, flour, sugar, bicarbonate of soda, baking powder, and salt. In a small bowl, whisk together buttermilk or milk, egg, and remaining 2 tablespoons oil. Stir buttermilk mixture into cornmeal mixture just until combined. Spoon batter into hot pans, filling wells three-fourths full. Bake until golden brown, 8 to 10 minutes. Let cool in pan for 5 minutes; serve warm.

Iced Lemon Cake

Serves 6-8
Prep time: 40 mins
Cook time: 35 mins

120g / ½ cup unsalted butter,
   room temperature
120g/ ⅝ cup caster/superfine sugar
2 large eggs
120g/ 1 cup self raising flour,
   sifted
1 tbsp lemon juice
1 tbsp grated lemon rind

ICING
180g/1 cup icing
   (powdered) sugar
3 tbsp lemon juice

Preheat oven to 190 C/375 F. Grease and line with greaseproof paper a small rectangular baking tin (23cm x12cm will do).

Cut the butter into small pieces and put in a food processor. Add the caster sugar and cream until blended, then drop in one egg. Process again, adding 1 tablespoon of flour, then drop in the second egg and process. Add the lemon rind, lemon juice and the rest of the flour and process once more. Turn the batter into the tin and bake for 35 minutes in the oven or until a skewer comes out clean from the middle. Allow to sit in the tin for 15 minutes, and then turn out onto a wire rack to cool.

ICING
Heat the lemon juice and when hot pour over the icing sugar and beat until it is the right thickness. Pour over the cake and smooth over the top and sides with a palette knife. A few curls of lemon rind over the top look attractive.

Chocolate Sponge Cake

Serves 6 - 8
Prep time: 60 mins
Cook time: 50 mins

210g/ 1 ½ cups plain flour
40g/ ½ cup cocoa powder
90g/ ½ cup brown sugar
150g/ ¾ cup caster/superfine sugar
1 tsp baking powder
½ tsp bicarbonate of soda
170g / ¾ cup melted butter
2 large eggs
1 tsp vanilla extract
120ml/ ½ cup buttermilk
120ml/ ½ cup hot water

CHOCOLATE ICING
115g / ½ cup unsalted butter
375g/3 cups icing/powdered sugar
100g/⅔ dark chocolate
1-2 tbsp milk
75g/½ cup chocolate chips

Preheat oven to 180 C/350 F. Grease and line a round 8 inch/20cm cake tin with baking paper.

In a large mixing bowl, add flour, cocoa powder, sugars, baking powder and bicarbonate of soda. In a separate bowl, add butter, eggs, vanilla and buttermilk and stir briefly. Add this to the dry ingredients mixture and stir to combine. Lastly add the hot water – it will make the batter quite thin which is correct. Pour batter into the tin and bake for 45-50 minutes. Leave on a wire rack to cool completely.

Icing: beat the butter in a large bowl until pale and creamy. Melt the chocolate in the microwave and set aside. Add half the sugar and 1 tbsp of milk to the butter and beat until combined. Add the remaining sugar and beat. Add the melted chocolate, and beat until smooth then ice the cake. Sprinkle over chocolate chips.

Molasses Gingerbread

Serves 6-8
Prep time: 1 hour
Cook time: 1 ½ hours

675g / 4 ½ cups plain flour
200g / 1 cup dark muscovado
   soft sugar
600g / 2 cups molasses
   or black treacle
250ml/1 cup buttermilk
   (or milk with 1 tbsp lemon juice)
3 large eggs
125ml/½ cup melted butter
2 teaspoons baking powder
1 teaspoon bicarbonate of soda
2 teaspoons ground ginger
2 teaspoons ground cinnamon
3 large tablespoons stem ginger
   with syrup
Pinch of salt

Preheat oven to 160 C/350 F. Grease and line with greaseproof paper a 23cm x 33cm baking tin.

Mix together in one bowl the flour, sugar, baking powder, bicarbonate of soda, spices and salt.

In another bowl mix the wet ingredients together, make a well in the dry ingredients and pour the wet mixture into it. Beat well to remove any lumps and pour the batter into the prepared tin.

Bake for at least an hour if not an hour and 15 minutes until the sides have come away from the tin, however the middle should be a little damp and sticky. Leave to cool in the tin and then turn out onto a flat surface and cut into squares.

Cinnamon Tea Cake

Serves 6 - 8
Prep time: 30 mins
Cook time: 30-35 mins

115g/½ cup butter at
   room temperature
150g/¾ cup caster/superfine sugar
1 tsp vanilla extract
2 large eggs
210g (1 & ½ cups) plain flour
2 ½ tsps baking powder
1 tsp ground cinnamon
180ml/¾ cup whole milk

CINNAMON SUGAR TOPPING
20g/1 tablespoon butter, melted
½ tsp ground cinnamon
1 tbsp caster sugar

This was a Langhorne household favourite and was baked individually like madeleines. This recipe has been adapted to one whole cake.

Preheat oven to 180 C/350 F. Grease and line a round 8 inch/20cm cake tin with baking paper.

In a large mixing bowl, beat the butter, sugar and vanilla with an electric mixer or handwhisk until pale. Add the eggs one at a time and beat. In a separate bowl, mix the flour, baking powder and cinnamon. Add half the flour and the milk and beat slowly, then add the remaining flour and beat slowly until smooth.

Pour the batter into the tin and bake for 30-35 minutes. Allow to cool for half an hour then extract from the tin. While it is still warm, brush with melted butter then sprinkle over the cinnamon and sugar.

Burnt House Cake

Serves 6-8
Prep time: 1 hour
Cook time: 1 ½ hours

BURNT SUGAR SYRUP
360g/ 1 ½ cups granulated/
   white sugar
180ml/ ¾ cup boiling water

BURNT SUGAR CAKE
240g/ 2 cups sifted plain flour
360g/ 1 ½ cups caster/superfine sugar
2 teaspoons baking powder
1 teaspoon salt
125ml/ ½ cup vegetable oil
7 large egg yolks
80ml/ ⅓ cup cooled burnt
   sugar syrup
60ml/ ¼ cup cold water
1 teaspoon pure vanilla extract
7 large egg whites
½ teaspoon cream of tartar

BURNT SUGAR ICING
435g/ 3 ½ cups icing/powdered sugar
113g/ ½ cup butter
7-8 tablespoons burnt sugar syrup
1 ½ teaspoon vanilla extract
1-2 tablespoons single cream

BURNT SUGAR SYRUP

In a heavy saucepan melt the sugar over a low heat until melted completely, stirring continuously. The mixture will be thick and a medium brown color when all the sugar is melted. Remove mixture from the heat and slowly whisk in the boiling water. The mixture will bubble (be very careful, the mixture is extremely hot). Set aside to cool completely and reserve for later use in the cake and icing. The syrup will thicken as it cools.

BURNT SUGAR CAKE

Preheat oven to 160 c/325°F. You will need a 25cm/10inch tube or Angel Cake pan.

Sift together flour, sugar, baking powder and salt in a large mixing bowl. Make a well in the flour mixture and add the ingredients in this order: cooking oil, unbeaten egg yolks, burnt sugar syrup, cold water and 1tsp vanilla extract. Stir ingredients together until just mixed and set aside.

Separately, in a large mixing bowl, with an electric beater, beat 7 large egg whites and ½teaspoon cream of tartar until egg whites form very stiff peaks. Pour the batter gradually over whipped egg whites, very gently folding it in with a spatula..Pour into the ungreased Angel cake tube pan and bake for 60-70 minutes. Remove cake from oven, and turn tube pan upside down over a glass bottle to cool. When cold, loosen all edges including around the center tube with a sharp knife and turn cake out of the pan onto a cake platter.

BURNT SUGAR ICING

Cream softened butter with electric mixer until pale and beat in a quarter of the icing sugar, and then another quarter. Stir in 7-8 tablespoons burnt sugar syrup, then beat in remaining icing sugar. Add the vanilla extract and 1-2 tablespoons half and half or cream. Ice the cake all over with a palette knife, allow to harden and serve.

Coconut Macaroons

Makes about 20 golfball size
Prep time: 20 mins
Cook time: 30 mins

200g/ 1 cup unsweetened
   desiccated coconut
200g/ ¾ cup sweetened
   condensed milk
1 tsp good quality vanilla extract
3 large egg whites at room
   temperature
¼ tsp salt

Preheat oven to 160 C/350 F. Grease and line with 2 oven trays with greaseproof paper. Combine the desiccated coconut, condensed milk and vanilla extract in a large bowl.

Whip the egg whites with the salt on high speed either with an electric handwhisk or mixer, until they form medium-firm peaks. Carefully fold the egg whites into the coconut mixture.

Mould with your hands into golfball shaped sizes (wet your hands if the mixture becomes a little dry). Bake for 25-30 minutes until golden brown.

Ginger Snaps

Makes about 30
Prep time: 20 mins +
20 mins careful rolling up
Cook time: 10-12 mins

120g/ ½ cup unsalted butter
120g/ ⅝ cup caster/superfine sugar
120g/ ½ cup golden syrup
   (or corn syrup)
120g/ 1 cup plain flour, sifted
   and warmed
1 ½ tbsp ground ginger
1 or 1½ tbsp lemon juice

GARNISH
275ml/ 1 ¼ cup whipped cream
1 tbsp vanilla sugar
   (or 1 tbsp caster sugar
   and 1 tsp brandy)

Preheat oven to 180 C/355 F. Grease 2 oven trays.

Melt butter, sugar and syrup, add the warmed flour, ginger and lemon. Stir well and drop onto on the well greased oven trays in teaspoonfuls, 15cm apart. Bake until golden brown, leave for a few moments to cool, then roll up over the thick handle of a wooden spoon. Leave to cool completely.

When cold, fill with the whipped cream. (If the rolling proves too time consuming, serve as thin ginger biscuits).

Sugardrop Cookies

Makes about 20
Prep time: 30 mins
Cook time: 10-12 mins

300g/ 2.5 cups plain flour
115g/ ½ cup unsalted butter
115g/ ½ cup lard or shortening
200g/ 1 cup caster/superfine sugar
1 egg
½ tsp baking powder
¾ tsp salt
1 tsp vanilla extract
2 tbps milk

Preheat oven to 150 C/300 F. Grease and line with 2 oven trays with greaseproof paper. Make sure all fridge ingredients are at room temperature.

In a bowl sift together flour, baking soda and salt; set aside.

In a large bowl, cream together butter, shortening, caster sugar and vanilla. Add egg and mix until fluffy. Stir in dry ingredients until mixture is smooth. Blend in milk. Drop by tablespoonfuls onto prepared sheet. Flatten with bottom of glass which has been dipped in more caster sugar. Bake for 10-12 minutes. (You can alter the flavor of the biscuits by adding lemon or almond or orange extracts each time).

Shortbread Biscuits (Cookies)

Makes about 20
Prep time: 30 mins
Cook time: 30 mins

110g/ ½ cup unsalted butter
50g/ ¼ cup caster/superfine sugar
175g/ 1 ⅜ cups plain flour

Preheat oven to 150 C/300 F. Grease and line with 2 oven trays with greaseproof paper.

Beat the butter until soft using an electric handwhisk or electric mixer, then beat in the sugar and finally the flour. Stop the mixer and bring the mixture together in the bowl using your hands, until you have a round ball of paste.

Lightly dust a surface with caster sugar and then roll it out until it's about 3mm thick. Cut the biscuits into whichever shape you want, rolling it out each time you have used it up. Place on the baking trays and cook for 30 minutes.

Cool the biscuits on a wire rack, dust them with caster sugar. Store them in an airtight container to keep them fresh.

'Those Thin Cookies'

Makes: about 30-40
Prep time: 30 mins plus
overnight refigeration
Cook time: 10 mins or less

200g/ 1 cup caster/superfine sugar
200g/ 1 cup soft light brown sugar
225g/ 1 cup unsalted butter
2 eggs
437g/ 3.5 cups plain flour
1 tsp baking powder
75g/ ½ cup chopped almonds
   or pecans

"Our cook was called Johnson, and there was a man who was always in and out of the cook's room. No one ever knew what that relationship was, but Johnson was a good cook and it was maybe one of those things best winked at."
Nancy Astor.

Originally known as 'ice box cookies' the method of refrigerating the dough overnight enabled Johnson to slice them extremely thinly. Nancy's older sister, the beauty Irene Gibson, always asked for 'those thin cookies' when she came to stay.

Cream together the butter and sugar until light and fluffy.

Beat the eggs with a fork and add to the butter and sugar mixture bit by bit, beating in between until the eggs are absorbed.

Beat in the flour and baking powder and lastly fold in the chopped nuts.

Knead well and shape into a roll, wrap in clingfilm and leave in the fridge overnight. (These also freeze extremely well, so can be prepared well in advance or simply stored for use later on).

The next day, preheat the oven to 220 C/395 F.

Lightly grease or oil a flat baking tray.

Slice the dough as thinly as possible and bake for 10 minutes or until golden brown. Keep a sharp eye on them as being so thin, they cook extremely quickly.

CHAPTER 6

NANCY LANCASTER

"Southern hospitality started because people lived deep in the country, separated from each other by miles and miles of impassable roads. They were so lonely that when they saw people going by they'd say, 'Damn it, stranger, stop and have a drink or I'll shoot you.' "

DRINKS & APÉRITIFS

'*There is an unwritten law of the British Constitution; you have to do what Royalty asks. Years later, the Duke of Kent said to me, "What are you going to do when my brother asks you to meet Mrs Simpson?" "She comes from Maryland, I come from Virginia," I told him, "She would soon as meet a rattlesnake as me."*' Nancy Astor, 1935.

There were two subjects on which Nancy Astor and her niece disagreed. One was the threat of a Second World War, which the Astors hoped to avoid if at all possible (the Trees supported more aggressive opposition to Nazi expansionism). The other was alcohol.

Both had grown up with Chillie Langhorne's lavish hospitality at Mirador, where, as Nancy Lancaster said, "Before lunch everyone sat under the trees, and if it was hot, there were Mint Juleps for which he was famous. We children

carried the glasses back to the pantry and always drained the dregs for the sugar, and I shudder to think of the many old moustaches I shared a glass with' Alcohol was to have tragic consequences for her uncles, the Langhorne brothers, Keene, Buck and Harry, whose drinking frequently got them into trouble and led to their early deaths. Nancy Astor's experiences with her brothers and her first husband, Robert Gould Shaw II, motivated her to spend considerable energy in Parliament to mitigating the negative effects of drink, particularly on women and children.

Although Nancy and Waldorf Astor were committed teetotalers, alcohol was not absent from their entertaining. At dinner the Astors always served extremely fine wines. Once, in 1923, when King George V and Queen Mary were guests of honour, the King's equerry took the Astors' butler, Mr Lee, to one side and handed him two decanters of port and sherry. When dinner was over Mr Lee quietly handed back the full decanters declaring 'Hardly necessary, I think you'll agree, sir.'

The Trees' houses were known for the wine, champagne and cocktails served at lunch and dinner, a deciding factor in Winston Churchill's selection of Ditchley as an alternative to Chequers during the war. He would consume a pint of either Pol Roger champagne or wine at lunch, often whiling away the rest of the afternoon with brandy and cigars. Although he loathed cocktails, the Mirador Cookbook gave up the intoxicating secrets of Chillie's Mint Juleps, Cherry Cobblers and Old Fashion's for the numerous other guests who loved them.

The war was won but many things were lost in the winning, including Ronnie and Nancy's marriage. In 1942 Nancy suffered a breakdown, after years of entertaining, her war work and missing Mirador, and moved out. Ronnie bought her the decorating firm of Colefax & Fowler where she and John Fowler were to continue their spectacularly successful partnership for many years. After a brief marriage to Jubie Lancaster, the owner of Kelmarsh and a short spell back at the house she adored, she purchased her final house, Haseley Court in Oxfordshire in 1954. This was her swansong, the last big house she decorated for herself or for anyone else, with the gardens she designed being of particular note. The sudden deaths of both parents, traumas of her broken marriages and the overwhelming burden of Ditchley were over. "In my early life Mirador was the healing thing for me, the balm; it healed all of my early ills. It always had that effect on me. Haseley was the same for me later in life. Haseley too had the power to heal whatever ailed me."

Her aunt Nancy Astor, now widowed, visited frequently, as did her sister Alice and brother-in-law Reginald Winn. "It was a marvellously comfortable, welcoming house and we adored her" says Jane Churchill, "and she always let us look at her jewellery. My sister Melissa spotted a piece and said, "that's very pretty Aunt Nancy, who gave you that?" Aunt Nancy gave her a sideways look and said "Ah'm not tellin' you...Ah've had three husbands and a very full life.""

OPPOSITE: Nancy Lancaster in the garden at Haseley Court, photographed by the great Valerie Finnis in 1959.

Bosom Caresser

Yolk of one egg
½ wine glass Curacoa
½ wine glass Brandy
1 wine glass good Madeira
   or good sherry
Roughly crushed ice
1 cocktail shaker

This cocktail brings to mind Nancy Lancaster, holding out her arms and reciting:

"Come into my arms, you bundle of charms,
And let me with enthusiasm, squeeze you to my boosiasm."

As with all the cocktail recipes brought over from Mirador, this was was extremely potent, and its provenance dates back to the late 1800s. The slightly inappropriate name may have something to do with the fact that these were served with the dessert or pudding course, and something that the ladies – who didn't otherwise drink alcohol – could partake in. Perhaps the gentlemen present were hoping this might propel all the ladies into their arms....who knows?

Fill the cocktail shaker with the crushed ice, pour over all the ingredients.

Shake well, pour into a pre-chilled glass and serve very cold.

Mint Julep

Makes: 1
Prep time: 5 minutes

65ml bourbon
10 mint leaves
1 sugar lump
Cracked ice
Spring of mint
1 highball glass
1 long handled spoon

"There is nothing in this world like sitting down, drinking a mint julep and looking out over your own land." Nancy Lancaster

Put in the lump of sugar into the bottom of the glass and water enough to melt it. Once melted put in the mint leaves and mash together hard. Crack some ice very fine and fill the glass. Keep glass dry on the outside. Pour in the bourbon, stir together then put the sprig of mint in the side to garnish.

Old Fashion'

Makes: 1
Prep time: 5 minutes

75ml bourbon whisky
1 lump sugar
A dash of bitters
2 tsp lemon juice
1 piece of lemon peel
1 piece orange peel
Sprig of mint
Ice cubes

An Old Fashion' (the Langhornes never pronounced the final '-ed') mixed by Collins the Ditchley butler, was guaranteed to kick off any party.

Put the lump of sugar in the bottom of heavy based tumbler. Add a few drops of bitters to the sugar and a little lemon juice squeezed over it. Put in the twists of lemon and orange peel , lumps of ice and finally the whisky poured over. Stir.

Mirador Cherry Cobbler

Makes: 1
Prep time: 5 mins

3 tbsp Rye Whiskey
1 ½ tbsp Cherry Syrup
   (see recipe below)
5-6 pitted cherries
Crushed Ice
Cinnamon Stick
Sprig of Mint

SYRUP
235ml/ 1 cup water
200g/ 1 cup sugar
225g/ 1 cup pitted fresh cherries
Juice of half a lime
Juice of one whole lemon
2 tablespoons grenadine

In a shallow, round, stemmed glass, place the cherries in the bottom. Mix whiskey and syrup with half of the crushed ice gently to combine. Pour into the glass. Pack more ice on top. Crush the sprig of mint slightly to release the oil and garnish the drink. Grate fresh cinnamon on top and use a straw to drink it.

To make the syrup, combine the first three ingredients in a saucepan over high heat. Bring to a boil. Remove from heat, cover and let sit for two hours. Strain solids from liquids and add next three ingredients to mix. Stir to combine. Pour into a clean, sterilized bottle. If not using immediately, add a generous splash of vodka to mix, or leave out vodka if using within 2 weeks.

The Maiden's Undoing

Makes: 1
Prep time: 5 mins

45ml dry gin
20ml orange Curacao liqueur
10ml lemon juice
5ml Grenadine syrup
2.5ml sugar syrup
1 round coupe glass
1 cocktail shaker

Fill the cocktail shaker with ice, add all the ingredients to it and shake well. Fine strain into a chilled coupe glass, and add a twist of lemon peel to garnish.

Hot Apple Cider Toddy

300ml/ 10 fl oz still apple cider
2 cinnamon sticks
2 star anise
8 whole cloves
1 ½ tablespoon of honey
100ml/ 4 fl oz whisky,
   rum or brandy
1 tablespoon lemon juice

In a saucepan, combine apple cider, cinnamon, star anise, and cloves. Bring to a boil. Remove from heat and cover with a lid. Allow spices to steep for 10-15 minutes.

Strain spices. Stir in honey to dissolve. Add whisky and lemon juice. Stir to combine. Add more honey according to taste, if desired. Serve with sliced apples, sliced lemons, cinnamon sticks, and star anise.

Light Dragoon Punch

Serves: 20
Prep time: 10 mins

800g/4 cups of granulated/white
   sugar
Juice of two dozen lemons
3 litres/4 quarts of California
   brandy
1 litre/1 quart of Jamaica rum
500ml/½ pint of peach brandy
Peel of six lemons
   (cut in slivers or curls)
Carbonated water

'Originally from Charleston in South Carolina this punch is named after a Confederate cavalry company, originally founded in 1792 as a city militia, who were more socialites than soldiers, drawn from Charleston's most prestigious families of planters, merchants and politicians. The punch was their drink of choice whenever the company was gathered. Stationed close to home they were a conspicuous component of cotillions and balls, and avoided much of the early fighting in the Civil War. Their baptism of fire came at the Battle of Haw's Shop in Hanover County, Virginia, where they fought with reckless bravery and suffered heavy losses. By 1865 only a handful of men survived and the company was disbanded.

Some recipes add 4 quarts of black tea to the ingredients below but there is no such dilution in my grandmother's receipt'. Isabella Tree.

In a large punchbowl, the liquids are mixed in the order given, and sparkling water is added just before serving.

Lady Adair's Mulled Claret

Serves: 10
Prep time: 10 mins

2 bottles of claret/red Bordeaux
½ bottle of brandy
¾ bottle of Kummel
1 glass of rum
¼ lemon
5-6 cloves
100g soft brown sugar

Combine all the ingredients in a large pan and heat very slowly on the stove, but do not boil. When sugar is absorbed, switch off the heat, transfer to a large silver tureen and serve.

Cranberry Elderflower Champagne Punch

Serves: 16
Prep time: 5 mins

180ml/ ¾ cup elderflower liqueur
360ml/ 1 ½ cups cranberry juice
120ml/ ½ cup lemon juice
120ml/ ½ cup sugar water
1 x 750ml bottle Prosecco
360ml/1 ½ cups club soda
Seasonal fruit, or cranberries,
   or citrus slices; for garnish

In a large jug, combine the elderflower liqueur, cranberry and lemon juices, and sugar water. Stir well and refridgerate overnight. When it's time to serve, pour the mixture into a punchbowl and add the sparkling wine and soda. Garnish with the fresh fruit and serve.

Iced 'Tea' Punch

Serves: 4
Prep time: 5 mins

50ml vodka
50ml dry gin
50ml tequila
50ml rum
50ml triple sec
50-100ml fresh lime juice
Crushed ice
500ml cola
2 limes cut into wedges

Pour the vodka, gin, tequila, rum and triple sec into a large jug, and add the lime juice. Fill half the jug with ice, then stir until the outside feels cold. Add the cola, stir to combine and drop in the lime wedges. Pour into tall glasses and serve.

Cider Cup

Serves: 4
Prep time: 10 mins

1 bottle of still cider
2 bottles of soda or
    sparkling water
1 sherry glass of brandy
1 lemon
Sprig of borage or slice
    of cucumber
Sugar or sugar lumps if using
    dry cider

Cider Cup was the only alcoholic drink Nancy Astor would serve at meals at Cliveden. Compared with a punch it was so diluted, she felt, as to be almost harmless.

Peel thinly one lemon and put the peel with a sprig of borage or a slice of cucumber in the cider. Add the brandy at once and the soda water 10 minutes later. If very dry cider is used add a few lumps of sugar. Ice but do not put ice in the cup.

White Wine, Peach & Mango Sangria

Serves: 16
Prep time: 10 mins

1 x 750ml bottle Pinot Grigio
  (or other dry white wine)
300ml/ 1¼ cups mango rum
300ml/ 1¼ cups peach schnapps
3 tablespoons lemon juice
3 tablespoons lime juice
3 tablespoons orange juice
600ml/ 2½ cups lemon-lime soda
Peach slices, garnish
Mango slices, garnish

Into a punch bowl or large jug, pour the wine, mango rum, peach schnapps, citrus juices and lemon-lime soda. Add lots of ice and mix well. Serve in glasses garnished with peach and mango slices.

Pimm's

50ml Pimm's No 1
150ml fizzy lemonade/Sprite or 7-Up
Strawberry, orange slices,
    cucumber, mint
Ice
1 highball glass

Fill the highball glass with ice, then pour in the Pimm's, followed by the lemonade and then the fruit and mint. Stir and serve.

'The Doctor'

1 part fresh lime juice
2 part sugar syrup
3 parts rum (White Bacardi)
4 parts water
Crushed ice
Cocktail shaker

Pour all the ingredients into a cocktail shaker filled with ice. Shake, strain and pour into a tall glass, with a few lumps of extra ice.

Sangria

2 oranges, chopped
2 pears, chopped
2 lemons, 1 chopped
    and 1 squeezed
200g red berries, chopped
    (e.g. raspberries, strawberries,
    cherries)
3 tablespoons caster/superfine sugar
1 teaspoon cinnamon
Ice
750ml/25 fl oz bottle light
    red wine
100ml/4 fl oz Spanish brandy
300ml/10 fl oz sparkling water

Put the chopped fruit in a bowl, sprinkle over the sugar and cinnamon, then stir to coat. Cover and leave to macerate in the fridge for at least 1 hour, or ideally overnight.

Fill a large jug or punchbowl with ice. Stir the macerated fruit mixture to ensure the sugar is dissolved, then tip into the jug or bowl with the wine and brandy. Stir, then top up with the sparkling water and serve.

Limeflower Cordial

Makes: 1 litre
Prep: 20 mins plus overnight infusion

1 litre/ 4 ¼ cups water
250-300g limeflower clusters
    (about half a carrier bag
    loosely packed)
500g/ 2 ½ cups caster/superfine sugar
5-10g citric acid

Lime flowers are the blossoms of the European Linden tree which flower in late spring.

Remove the lime flowers from their stalks, and put them into a bowl big enough for the water. Boil the water and pour it over the flowers, cover with a teatowel and leave to infused overnight or for at least 8 hours. Strain through a sieve lined with muslin or a jelly bag, and allow this to happen naturally.

Bring the infusion to a simmer in a saucepan with the sugar and citric acid, until the sugar has dissolved. Boil for 5 minutes, then bottle in sterilized, warmed bottles and keep refrigerated for up to a month.

Mint Fruit Punch

Serves: 12
Prep time: 20 mins plus 2-3 hours chilling time

1 large cucumber, peeled and
    chopped into small chunks
small bunch mint, leaves stripped
juice of 6 limes plus extra wedges
    to serve
200g/ ¾ cup caster/superfine sugar
1-2 small melons: honeydew,
    cantaloupe, watermelon
10 strawberries
1 litre sparkling water

Put the cucumber and half the mint into a large bowl or jug with the lime juice and sugar. Leave to infuse for at least two hours in the refrigerator.

Using a melon baller, scoop out as many melon balls from the three varieties of melon, add to the jug and leave again for 30 minutes. Top up with sparkling water, add the sliced strawberries, mint leaves and lime wedges and serve.

Iced Coffee Frappé

Makes: 1
Prep time: 10 mins

120ml/ ½ cup espresso or
    instant espresso (cooled)
A large handful icecubes
60ml/ ¼ cup milk
2 tbsp sugar to taste

Put all the ingredients in an electric blender, starting on a low speed to break the ice cubes gently. Increase the speed and blend on high for 30 seconds until smooth. Pour into a tall glass and serve.

Moroccan Mint Tea

Serves: 4
Prep time: 10 mins

Green tea leaves, 1 tsp per person
Sugar, 1 tsp per person
A handful of fresh mint

Boil a kettle and warm a teapot with a small amount before pouring it out. Add the green tea leaves, sugar and mint then fill the teapot with boiling water. Leave to brew for about 10 minutes then serve using a strainer.

Lemon Barley Water

Makes: 1.2 litres
Prep time: 20 mins

150g/ ¾ cup pearl barley
2 medium lemons, zested
   and squeezed
1.2L/ 5 cups water
120ml/ ½ cup runny honey

Rinse the barley in sieve under the tap, then put in a large saucepan with the lemon zest and water. Bring to a boil and simmer for 10 minutes. Strain the mixture into a bowl, and add the honey and lemon juice and allow to cool. Bottle and refrigerate until needed.

Pussy Foot Cup

Makes: about 2.75 litres
Prep time: 10 mins

1 litre fizzy lemonade/Sprite or 7-Up
450ml dry ginger ale
450ml tonic water
450ml soda water or
   sparkling mineral water
175ml orange juice
175ml lemon juice
1 green apple, unpeeled,
   quartered, cored and sliced
Peel of ¼ cucumber
3 large sprigs mint
A few strawberries

Mix all together and serve in a large jug with ice.

Mrs Gibson's Iced Tea

8 tablespoons (45g) Indian
   tea leaves such as Assam or
   Darjeeling
4 tablespoons sugar
Juice of 1 lemon
Juice of 3 oranges
Approx.. 825ml ginger ale
   (optional)
Lemon slices
Sprigs of mint
570ml iced water
Plenty of ice cubes

Named for Irene Gibson, elder sister of Nancy Astor, and Nancy Lancaster's aunt, who was a noted beauty and the inspiration for her husband Charles Gibson's creation 'The Gibson Girl'. This was an iconic representation of the beautiful and independent Euro-American woman at the turn of the 20th century. This recipe for Iced Tea quickly became a favourite alternative to the much blander lemon barley water found at tennis teas and garden parties.

Put the 8 tablespoons of tea leaves in a large pan. Pour over 1.2 litres of boiling water. Add sugar, stir well. Squeeze the juice of the lemon and oranges and pour it through a sieve or colander filled with ice cubes. Strain the tea over ice cubes as well and add to the juices. Add 570ml of iced water and put in the fridge to chill.

"I pour it over ice cubes in tall glasses, adding half as much ginger ale just before serving, and garnish with lemon slices and sprigs of mint." Nancy Lancaster.

ACKNOWLEDGEMENTS

The authors would like to thank the following for their help, support and encouragement, in providing extraordinarily beautiful props to illustrate the recipes: Carole Bamford and Daylesford Organic, www.daylesford.com Insta @daylesfordfarm, the team at Cabana Magazine www.cabanamagazine.com Insta @cabanamagazine, Isabella Tree at Knepp Castle www.knepp.co.uk Insta @isabellatree, Libby Blakey Design www.libbyblakeydesign Insta @libbyblakeyinteriors, Samantha Godsal www.cobblerscove.com Insta @cobblerscovehotel, Carole Langton www.langtontextiles.co.uk Insta @langtontextiles, Alice Naylor-Leyland, www.mrsalice.com Insta @mrsalice, Anne Singer www.annesingercollection.com Insta @annesingercollection, Rebecca Udall www.rebeccaudall.com Insta @rebeccaudallhome, William Yeoward www.williamyeowardcrystal.com Insta @williamyeoward and finally, Paul Raben. Many thanks to Pulbrook & Gould London, www.pulbrookandgould.co.uk Insta @pulbrookandgould for the exquisite flower arrangements and Tracey Morgan Spokes www.onceupon-atime.co.uk Insta @flowerstory13 for the gorgeous arrangements at Kelmarsh Hall.

A huge debt of gratitude is owed to the locations where we were able to photograph: The Ditchley Foundation, Kerry and James Arroyo and their staff at Ditchley Park www.ditchley.com, Ian and Natalie Livingstone and all the staff at Cliveden www.clivedenhouse.co.uk Insta @clivedenhouse, The National Trust www.nationaltrust.org.uk Insta @cliveden_national_trust which manages the Cliveden gardens to perfection, Lesley Denton, Eleanor and Estelle at Kelmarsh Hall www.kelmarsh.com Insta @kelmarshhall and Henry Wyndham. You all made us feel so welcome and not as if we were in the way at all, which of course we were...

More thanks are owed to those who helped us track down obscure photographs, anecdotes and old newspaper clippings, or just allowed us to look through their archives, these include the Astor Archive at the University of Reading www.collections.reading.ac.uk, Isabella Tree, Henry Wyndham and Trudi Ballard at Colefax & Fowler www.colefax.com Insta @colefaxandfowler. Finally, this book would not look the way it does without an extraordinary contribution from Andrew Montgomery who shot all the photography, www.andrewmontgomery.co.uk Insta @montgomeryphoto, Charlotte Heal who designed all the pages www.charlotteheal.com Insta @charlottehealdesign and Jake McConville who cooked and styled all the recipes www.jakeskitchen.co.uk Insta @jakeskitchen. To Bob Colacello Insta @bobcolacello for kindly writing the foreword, to Patrick Green QC for the loan of his hipflask and silver ladle and overall encouragement, and of course the team at Clearview Books www.clearviewbooks.com Insta @clearviewcatharinesnow for bringing it all together, many many thanks to you all.

Jane Churchill & Emily Astor